Doug McPhillips - Other Visionary Stories

NOVELS
From Darkness to Light
Awake to my gutted dreams
The Sword of Discernment
Santiago Traveller
I, Prophet
The Guru of Jerusalem
Masters at my table
We Are Me Upside Down (Autobiography)
The Wicklow Way
The Adventures of Ace McDice,
Stretch Deed & Moonshine Melody
Instant Karma & Grace
The Credo
Reflections of an Old Man
A Writer on the Rocks (Autobiography)
Reincarnation of the Assassin
The One
Master of the Arts
Masters of Introspection
The songs, not the Singer
To Whom It May Concern
A Camino Guidebook.

ALBUMS

Country Camino
Santiago Traveller
Soul Fact

© Doug McPhillips 2024. ISBN : 978-0-6486214-9-2

This book is copyrighted. Except for fair dealings for private study, research, criticism, or review, as permitted under the Copyright Act, no part may be reproduced by any process without the editor's written permission.

National Library of Australia Catalogue—in-publication data: The author's references throughout this book, Google research on myth, legend, and folklore.

Mein Kampf, Adolf Hitler, Penguin Press- 1992.
The Rise and Fall of the Third Reich- Connell Publishing- Julian Fellowes-2016
The Rise of the Fourth Reich, William Morrows,- Jim Marrs-2023.
Research on Secret World Government- Author's Identity- protected. 2024.
Towers of Basel- Shadows of Secret Bank- Google Books- 2013.
Social Change and Political Development in Weimar Germany, Richard Blessey- London- 1981.

This book is a work of both fact and fiction. Not all the characters in this novel are accurate. Where fiction resembles actual events, locales, or persons, living or dead, it is entirely coincidental. When poetic licence turns fact into fiction, names have been changed to protect the innocent.

It may also be noted that apart from the research I have undertaken via Google and other sources for this book, much of the written references are the remarkable work of Jim Mars in his efforts to write his aforementioned book. Throughout this writing, my references for direct quotes and other comments about his work are denoted by an asterisk symbol (*).

Content.

Prologue.   Page 5.

Chapter 1. Young Adolf. Page 7.

Chapter 2. The Power of Nazi Ideology. Page 15.

Chapter 3. The Rise of a Fourth Reich. Page 29.

Chapter 4.   Endless Shades of Grey. Page 37.

Chapter 5. The Men Behind the Throne. Page 47.

Chapter 6. The Rule of Terror. Page 57.

Chapter 7. Germany under the 3rd Reich. Page 67

Chapter 8. The Mission of World Dominion. Page 73.

Chapter 9. The Redemption of a Radical Priest. Page 85.

Chapter 10. The Second Coming of Donald Trump. Page 91.

Chapter 11. A Pawn in the game. Page 99.

Chapter 12. To Live and let die. Page 109.

Chapter 13. The Bankers behind the Throne. Page.119.

Chapter 14. A Repeat of Historical Dictatorships Page 127.

Chapter 15. The Kremlin Powerhead.   Page. 137.

Chapter 16. Totalitarian World Rulers.   Page. 149.

Chapter 17. The Parallels of History. Page 159.

Chapter 18. Rules of Church and State.Page 169.

Chapter 19. United We Stand.Page 177.

Chapter 20. The Propaganda machine. Page 189.

Chapter 21. Epilogue. Page 195.

Prologue

The Holy Roman Empire had survived over a thousand years when it was finally destroyed by Napoleon and the French in 1806. It may not have been holy or Roman or an empire, as Voltaire remarked, but whatever it was, it had survived for more than a thousand years since the coronation of Charlemagne in the year 800.

The holy realm of the European Empire rose after the fall of the former era of the emperors of Rome from Caesar Augustus to Hadrian. The new Empire was known as The First Reich, and Charlemagne, king of the Franks, was crowned "Emperor of the Romans" by Pope Leo III in 800 CE, thus restoring the Roman Empire in the West for the first time since its dissolution in the 5th century. Charlemagne was selected for various reasons, including his long-standing protectorate over the papacy. The rule structure of this first Reich dominated Western Europe from 800 until 1806 when Napoleon defeated it.

The Second Reich: All of Germany was united behind Prussia under the leadership of Otto von Bismarck, the victor of the Franco-Prussian War. It was called Imperial Germany, the Second Reich, or simply Germany. The period of the German Reich was from the unification of Germany in 1871 until the November Revolution in 1918 when the German Reich changed its form of government from a monarchy to a republic. Only the defeat of Germany in World War 1 broke the power of this second German empire. And then, in 1933, Adolf Hitler was appointed Chancellor of Germany after convincing other members of the Reichstag that the Nazi party was better for the country than their feared rivals, the Communists. Within the year, the President of the German Republic died, and Hitler declared himself supreme leader of Germany. The world trembled as the Third Reich: Adolf Hitler, Nazi Germany, World War II, and what was thought to be the Last German Empire arose with a devastating plan to rule the world for one thousand years. This book examines the history of the Reich that led constitution of the Weimar Republic and the Treaty of Versailles and comes to understand why Hitler believed it was crucial to build a new Nazi empire that was second to no one other nation in Europe in terms of military development. We learn how Hitler used the rhetoric of racism and nationalism to transform himself from a democratically elected member of government into a dictator whose word was law. Most importantly, you'll learn how those changes paved the way for World War II and the atrocities of the Holocaust.

The writer herein examines the chronicle of events that led to Hitler's rise and fall and the aftermath that existed since the fall, the death of Hitler and the Nazi regime. This aftermath has since brought about the rise of a Fourth Reich in the 20th and 21st centuries. The story is told partly from fiction but mainly from historical facts and present-day details of the 'Empire of the Western World' that may be the way of the future if we are not attuned to do our part to bring about change for the betterment of humanity.

CHAPTER 1.

YOUNG ADOLF

Adolf Hitler was born on April 20, 1889, at Braunau am Inn, Austria. He was the founder and leader of the Nazi Party from 1920 to the time of his death in 1945. Hitler's worldview revolved around two concepts: territorial expansion on 30th April 1945 becoming Chancellor and Fuhrer of Germany from 1933 and racial supremacy. Those themes informed his decision to invade Poland, which marked the start of World War 11, as well as the systematic killing of six million Jews and millions of others during the Holocaust. Hitler's father, Alois (born 1837), was illegitimate. For a time, he bore his mother's name, Schicklgruber, but by 1876, he had established his family claim to the surname Hitler. Adolf never used any other surname.

After his father retired from the state customs service, Adolf Hitler spent most of his childhood in Lintz, the capital of Upper Austria. It remained his favourite city, and he wished to be buried there. The Father Alois Hitler died in 1903 but left an adequate pension and savings to support his wife and children. Although Hitler feared and disliked his father, he was a devoted son to his mother, who died after much suffering in 1907. With a mixed record as a student, Hitler only advanced up to a secondary education.. After leaving school, he visited Vienna and returned to Linz, where he dreamed of becoming an artist. Later, he used the small allowance he continued to draw to maintain himself in Vienna. He wished to study art, for which he had some capability, but he failed to secure entry to the Academy of Fine Arts twice. For some years, he lived a lonely and isolated life, earning a precarious livelihood by painting postcards and advertisements while drifting from one municipal hostel to another. Hitler already showed traits that characterised his later life.

In 1913, Hitler moved to Munich. He had applied for Austrian Military service in February 1914 but was classified as unfit because of inadequate physical vigour. However, when World War 1 broke out, he petitioned Bavarian King Louis 111 to be allowed to serve, and one day after submitting that request, he was notified that he would be permitted to join the 16th Bavarian Reserve Infantry Regiment. After eight weeks of training, Hitler was deployed to Belgium in October 1914, where he participated in the First Battle of Ypres. He served throughout the war, was wounded in October 1916, and was gassed two years later near Ypres. He was hospitalised when the conflict ended. During the war, he was continuously in the front line as a headquarters runner; his bravery in action was rewarded with the Iron Cross, Second Class, in December 1914, and the Iron Cross, First Class (a rare decoration for a corporal), in August 1918. He greeted the war with enthusiasm, as a great relief from the frustration and the aimlessness of civilian life. He found discipline and comradeship satisfying, which was confirmed by his belief in the heroic virtues of war.

Intent on remaining in the army, having found a real purpose in life, Hitler was appointed to the Military Intelligence Propaganda section, where he undertook political training. His activities involved making speeches to the troops advocating German nationalism and non-socialism, where he developed further his oratory skills. He also acted as an army informer, spying on small political parties. He, at the time, joined the German Workers Party, an extreme anti-Communist, anti-Semitic right-wing organisation.

Hitler challenges Anton Drexler to become the leader of the Nazi party. After initial resistance, Drexler agrees, and Hitler becomes the party's new leader. And in 1923 Along with other right-wing factions and General Ludendorff, he attempted to overthrow the Bavarian government with an armed uprising. The event became known as The Beer Hall Putsch. Hitler and 2000 Nazis marched through Munich to the Beer Hall to take over a meeting chaired by three of the most critical individuals in Bavarian politics. Defendants in the Beer Hall Putsch trial, apart from Hitler, included

Pernet, Weber, Frick, Krieber, Ludendorff, Brucker, Rohm and Wagner.

The following day, the Nazis march in the streets, the police open fire. Hitler escapes but is captured, tried for treason and serves nine months in Landsberg prison. During his imprisonment, he began dictating his thoughts to Rudolf Hess, which emerged in the book *Mein Kampf* (My Struggle). It is a mixture of autobiography, political ideology and examining propaganda techniques.

In 1925, it became clear in his absence that only some people could create a successful ultra-right-wing movement. Upon Hitler's release from prison, he reconstitutes the Nazi Party under his exclusive leadership. The Party did very poorly in elections, but this period allowed Hitler to recruit a small but devoted group of followers, including many who would be leading figures in the Nazi regime after it came to power.

However, on his release from jail, his time and focus were only sometimes on Party issues. He held a great sway over young women and small children. Though no impropriety can be levelled at him, or at least proven, he did, however, influence the hearts and minds of those with whom he had known sexual encounters and certainly influenced their minds to take the ultimate step of death by suicide. There were six known suicidal deaths of young women attributed to having had an encounter of a sexual nature with him.

 He dated one Maria Reiter, 16 at the time, when he was 37. This was in 1925. While he is said to have made sexual advances at her, it would be totally in keeping with the morals of the time that she declined and that the dates were restricted to dinners. He also met Geli Raubal, his half-niece, in the same time frame; she was 17 when her mother became Hitler's housekeeper in 1925. She was accompanied by her daughter Geli. At first, all seemed well. Angela achieved financial stability while reconnecting with her brother, and Hitler was more than happy to step in as Geli's guardian.

They became close, and it's not hard to imagine why Hitler adored Geli and was incredibly generous: paying for singing lessons, taking her shopping, and even having her room specifically designed for her liking. Initially, this affection was reciprocated. However, things would soon begin to sour. The question which often arises is whether Hitler and Geli had a sexual relationship. While it is easy to speculate, such an accusation remains impossible to prove. What can be said with certainty is that Hitler loved his niece, but he did not love her well.

Hitler once told his driver Emil Maurice, who was fascinated with Geli, *"I love and could marry her. But you know what my viewpoint is. I want to remain single. So I retain the right to exert an influence on her circle of friends until such a time as she finds the right man..."*

Geli had been planning a trip to Vienna to meet up with a friend. It's believed that this "friend" may have been a man she planned on eloping with. Whether or not this was true, Geli became incredibly troubled by Hitler's last-minute decision to have her mother accompany her. Geli was distraught and pleaded with him that their relationship was tumultuous. While Hitler may have been able to offer her financial security, his controlling nature was suffocating. Geli was no longer the child who had visited Hitler at Landsberg Prison all those years ago. She desired freedom. Unfortunately, a woman's options were limited, with marriage being the most straightforward option. Her push to regain autonomy came from Hitler's driver, Emil Maurice. Had this been the worst incident it could be understood. After all, Maurice was more or less a violent gang member. It would be understandable for Geli's mother and Hitler not to want her to marry him. Unfortunately, this simply remains the most notable interference. As stated by Wilhelm Stocker, an SA officer who guarded Hitler's Munich apartment, "Many times when Hitler was away for several days. Geli would associate with other men. Hitler would have been furious if he had known that she was out with such men as a violin player from Augsburg or a ski instructor from Innsbruck. The pressure under which Geli lives is burdensome to her, and what makes matters worse is that she's prevented from saying how unhappy she feels." Heinrich Hoffmann speaking of Geli.

Contemporary witnesses reported that Hitler was overly possessive and domineering of her. When Hitler learned that she had begun a relationship with his chauffeur, Emil Maurice, he forbade her from ever seeing the man again and had Maurice transferred to another assignment. To state that he was "exerting an influence" would be an understatement. Unable to marry Geli himself and unwilling to allow anyone else the chance to do so, her life in Munich became increasingly limited. Having stepped in as her de facto father figure, Hitler deemed it his prerogative to dictate who she could and couldn't see. As a result, Geli was not allowed to leave his apartment unaccompanied. His severe vetting of friends limited her social circle in the city, and she was forced to sneak out if she wished to date. Such behaviour may have been more understandable had Geli been a teenager, but she was an adult now. What may have once been interpreted as protective now became overbearing. He restricted her from leaving the apartment.

Before he left on a trip to Nuremberg on September 18 1931, he and the then 23-year-old Raubal got into a heated argument during which Hitler forbade her from returning to her native Austria. The following day was found shot dead in Hitler's Munich apartment. She had taken her own life with one of Hitler's pistols. Their blowout appears to have been a breaking point. There have been persistent rumours that Geli Raubal was pregnant to Hitler at the time of her alleged suicide. It seems to have been the breaking point. At the age of twenty-three, Geli would take her own life using Hitler's Walther pistol.

After Geli's death, Hitler rarely spoke of her. This was not indifference on his part, and it was simply too painful for him to mention. On the occasions which he did, he would tear up. It's silly to think that her continued presence would have deterred his darkest inclinations. Still, the trauma of her death was too much to bear. The event received much coverage in German newspapers, including accusations of an incestuous relationship. Hitler had confided that Geli was the only person, aside from his mother, that he ever truly loved. Following Geli's death, Hitler became despondent, and those closest to him were afraid he might take his own life.

Around this time, Hitler's photographer, Heinrich Hoffman, introduced him to his young shop assistant, Eva Braun, hoping she might distract him from Geli. Eva Braun was also quite a bit younger than Hitler; she was 19 in 1931 when their relationship seemed to have started. Of course, at the time, it was much more familiar with significant age differences in couples than it is today. It would also not be considered outrageous that a girl of 16 was being courted with a view to marriage, even by a man twice her age. Whatever you it would still be legal today, as the age of consent is still 16 in Germany. Hitler had several relationships with women during his lifetime—two committed suicide. A third died of complications eight years after a suicide attempt, and a fourth also attempted suicide. And then there was Eva Braun. We all know what happened to her.

Hitler's only genuine affection seems to have been for his dog, Foxl, a white terrier that had strayed across from enemy lines. Hitler taught it tricks, revelling in how attached it was to him. It would be this same man who loved animals, cakes, children and alpine walks who would send millions to their deaths and believed sincerely that that was the right thing to do, that God or fate or providence had appointed him to save Germany and the German people.

Hitler created a public image of a celibate man without a domestic life, dedicated entirely to his political mission and the governance of Nazi Germany. His relationship with Eva Braun, which lasted nearly 14 years, was hidden from the public and all but his inner circle knew about it. Braun biographer Heike Görtemaker notes that the couple enjoyed an everyday sex life. Hitler and Braun married in late April 1945, less than 40 hours before committing suicide together. Hitler reportedly once spoke of a son. Nothing more was spoken of him except for the fact that a most potent dictator, 'Candidate to head of a Fourth Reich', who claimed Hitler was his grandfather, emerges in the fiction of this story.

There were rumours of a link with the Jewish elite and reportedly a member of the secret society of a One World Order had become a priest and theologian in Vatican City. Equally another story emerged that it was Hitler's grandson who became that priest but like all rumours, there are no facts to substantiate either story. It's what Donald Trump might call"Fake news." This writer in attempting to add a tinge of colour to an otherwise dull plot might please be forgiven for adding the viewpoint from the angle and lens of a non-existent man of the cloth. reported to be Hitler's grandson.

For a reminder of how the Third Reich and all of its power, ideology and historical outcomes came into being, we need to take a trip down the history's memory lane of the Reichs. It is necessary to align the facts with the novel's fiction that will come into play in the following chapters. For this author believes that a new wave of international insanity of the people of today, the 21st century, is rising again towards a Fourth Reich, which may be even more devastating for mankind than the former Third Reich of Adolf Hitler and the Nazi Regime.

CHAPTER 2.

POWER OF THE NAZI IDEOLOGY

To recap, The First Reich: Charlemagne, king of the Franks, is declared ruler of the Holy Roman Empire, which dominated western Europe from 800 until 1806, when Napoleon defeated it. The Second Reich: All of Germany is united behind Prussia under the leadership of Otto von Bismarck, victor of the Franco-Prussian War. Only Germany's defeat in World War I could break the power of the second German empire.

The Third Reich: In 1933, Adolf Hitler was appointed Chancellor of Germany after convincing other members of the Reichstag that the Nazi party was better for the country than their feared rivals, the Communists. Within the year, the President of the German Republic died, and Hitler declared himself the supreme leader of Germany. Hitler, with his rhetoric of racism and nationalism, transformed himself from a democratically elected member of government into a dictator whose word was law. Such a change as it was paved the way for World War II and the atrocities of the Holocaust.

So, to give an overview of what came to pass on December 10, 1870, the North German Confederation Reichstag renamed the Confederation the German Empire and gave William I, the King of Prussia, the title of German Emperor. The new constitution (Constitution of the German Confederation) and the title of Emperor came into effect on January 1, 1871. During the Siege of Paris on January 18, 1871, William accepted to be proclaimed Emperor in the Hall of Mirrors at the Palace of Versailles.

The Reichstag adopted the second German Constitution on April 14, 1871, and proclaimed by the Emperor on April 16. It was substantially based on Bismarck's North German Constitution. The political system remained the same. The empire had a parliament called the *Reichstag*, elected by universal male suffrage. However, the original constituencies drawn in 1871 were never redrawn to reflect the growth of urban areas. As a result, rural areas were grossly over-represented during the significant expansion of German cities in the 1890s and the first decade of the 20th century.

Legislation also required the consent of the *Bundesrat*, the federal council of deputies from the 27 states. Executive power was vested in the emperor, or *Kaiser*, who was assisted by a chancellor responsible only to him. The emperor was given extensive powers by the constitution. He alone appointed and dismissed the chancellor (which in practice was used by the emperor to rule the empire through him), was supreme commander-in-chief of the armed forces, the final arbiter of all foreign affairs, and could disband the *Reichstag* to call for new elections. Officially, the chancellor was a one-man cabinet and was responsible for all state affairs; in practice, the State Secretaries (bureaucratic top officials in charge of fields such as finance, war, foreign affairs, etc.) acted as unofficial portfolio ministers. The *Reichstag* had the power to pass, amend, or reject bills and initiate legislation. However, as mentioned above, the real power was vested in the emperor, who exercised it through his chancellor. Although nominally a federal empire and league of equals, in practice, the empire was dominated by the largest and most powerful state, Prussia. It stretched across the northern two-thirds of the new *Reich* and contained three-fifths of its population. The imperial crown was hereditary in the House of Hohenzollern, the ruling house of Prussia. Except for 1872–1873 and 1892–1894, the chancellor was always simultaneously the prime minister of Prussia. With 17 out of 58 votes in the *Bundesrat*, Berlin needed only a few votes from the small states to exercise effective control.

The other states retained their governments but had limited aspects of sovereignty, with new postage stamps and currency issued for the empire. The Parliament of Germany from 1871 to 1918 shared legislative powers with the *Bundesrat*, the Imperial Council of the reigning princes of the German States. It had no formal right to appoint or dismiss governments, but it was considered a highly modern and progressive parliament by contemporary standards. All German men over 25 were eligible to vote, and members were elected by general, universal, and secret ballot.

So it was that the last German Emperor, Wilhelm 11(Kaiser) and King of Prussia, ruled the German Empire and the Kingdom of Prussia from June 1888 to November 1918. He dismissed Chancellor Otto von Bismarck in 1890. He launched Germany on a bellicose "New Course" in foreign affairs, culminating in his support for Austria-Hungary in the crisis of July 1914, which led to World War 1. The German Empire (officially *Deutsches Reich*) was the historical German nation-state from Germany's unification in 1871 to Kaiser Wilhelm II's abdication in November 1918, when Germany became a federal republic (the Weimar Republic).

The German Empire comprised 26 constituent territories, most ruled by royal families. This included four kingdoms, six grand duchies, five duchies (six before 1876), seven principalities, three free Hanseatic cities, and one imperial territory. Although the Kingdom of Prussia contained most of the Empire's population and territory, it eventually played a relatively lesser political role. As Dwyer (2005) points out, Prussia's "political and cultural influence had diminished considerably" by the 1890s, after the era of Bismarck's leadership.

After Germany was united by Otto von Bismarck into the "German Reich," he dominated German politics until 1890 as Chancellor. Bismarck tried to foster alliances in Europe to contain France and consolidate Germany's influence in Europe. Bismarck's post-1871 foreign policy was conservative and sought to preserve the balance of power in Europe. British historian Eric Hobsbawm concludes that he "remained undisputed world champion at the game of multilateral diplomatic chess for almost twenty years after 1871, [devoting] himself exclusively, and successfully, to maintaining peace between the powers." His chief concern was that France would plot revenge after its defeat in the Franco-Prussian War. As the French lacked the strength to defeat Germany themselves, they sought an alliance with Russia that would trap Germany between the two in a war (as would ultimately happen in

1914). Bismarck wanted to prevent this and maintain friendly relations with the Russians, thereby allied with them and Austria-Hungary. The League of Three Emperors was signed in 1872 by Russia, Austria, and Germany. It stated that republicanism and socialism were common enemies and that the three powers would discuss any matters concerning foreign policy.

Bismarck's domestic policies played an important role in forging the authoritarian political culture of the new Empire. Less preoccupied with continental power politics following unification in 1871, Germany's semi-parliamentary government carried out a relatively smooth economic and political revolution from above that pushed them along the way to becoming the world's leading industrial power of the time.

Bismarck's "revolutionary conservatism" was a conservative state-building strategy designed to make ordinary Germans— not just the Junker elite—more loyal to the state and emperor. He planned to grant social rights to enhance the integration of a hierarchical society, forge a bond between workers and the state to strengthen the latter, maintain traditional authority relations between social and status groups, and provide a countervailing power against the modernist forces of liberalism and socialism. He created the modern welfare state in Germany in the 1880s, introduced health care and social security, and enacted universal male suffrage in the new German Empire in 1871. He became a great hero to German conservatives, who erected many monuments to his memory and tried to emulate his policies.

At the same time, Bismarck tried to reduce the political influence of the emancipated Catholic minority in the Kulturkampf, literally "culture struggle." The Catholics only grew stronger, forming the Center (*Zentrum*) Party. Germany overgrew in industrial and economic power, matching Britain by 1900. Its highly professional army was the best in the world, but the navy could never catch up with Britain's Royal Navy.

In 1888, the young and ambitious Kaiser Wilhelm II became emperor. He could not abide advice, least of all from the most experienced politician and diplomat in Europe, so he fired Bismarck. The Kaiser opposed Bismarck's careful foreign policy and wanted Germany to pursue colonialist policies as Britain and France had been doing for decades and build a navy that could match the British. The Kaiser promoted active colonisation of Africa and Asia for those areas that were not already colonies of other European powers; his record was notoriously brutal and set the stage for genocide. In what became known as the "First Genocide of the Twentieth-Century," between 1904 and 1907, the German colonial government in South-West Africa (present-day Namibia) ordered the destruction of the local Herero and Namaqua peoples as a punitive measure for an uprising against German colonial rule, killing over 100,000 people. The Kaiser took a mostly unilateral approach in Europe with the Austro-Hungarian Empire as its main ally, and an arms race with Britain eventually led to the assassination of the Austrian-Hungarian crown prince Archduke Franz Ferdinand, which sparked World War I.

After four years of warfare in which approximately two million German soldiers were killed, a general armistice ended the fighting on November 11, and German troops returned home. In the German Revolution (November 1918), Emperor Wilhelm II and all German ruling princes abdicated their positions and responsibilities, marking the beginning of the Weimar Republic.

Germany's new political leadership signed the Treaty of Versailles in 1919. In the German Revolution (November 1918), Emperor Wilhelm II and all German ruling princes abdicated their positions and responsibilities, marking the beginning of the Weimar Republic. Germany's new political leadership signed the Treaty of Versailles in 1919. The German Empire (officially Deutsche Reich) was the historical German nation state that existed from the unification of Germany in 1871 to the abdication of Kaiser Wilhelm 11 in November 1918 when Germany became a federal republic (the Weimar Republic).

The Weimar Constitution has been subjected to considerable criticism, notably for the system of proportional representation that it introduced and the large powers that it conferred on the president. For the first time in German history, however, it provided a firm foundation for democratic development. The fact that within 14 years, this ended in a dictatorship was due far more to the course of events and the character of social forces in Germany than to constitutional defects.

The German Reich, as it was re-established in 1919, was a democratic but not socialist republic. Several measures for socialising certain parts of the national economy (such as the coal, electricity, and potash industries) were introduced but proved ineffectual. German industry continued to be marked by cartels and other combines of a monopolistic character, control of which was increasingly concentrated in the hands of a few men. Because of the hopes aroused in 1918–19, no far-reaching plan for securing public control over industry or breaking up the big landed estates was carried through, which had two consequences. First, although the German working class undoubtedly improved its political and economic status under the republic, a considerable portion was embittered by the failure to effect drastic reform of the social and financial systems. This disenchantment was to provide the left-wing opposition with working-class solid support, which weakened both the Social Democratic Party and the republic. Second, economic power was left in the hands of those who were either irreconcilable opponents of the republic from the beginning or supporters of other parties with a preference for dictatorial forms of government.

The position of the trade unions, the eight-hour workday, and the right to collective bargaining were safeguarded under the republic, but the attempt to extend democracy to the industrial sphere met with powerful opposition from the industrialists. A works council set up early in 1920 enabled the workers in each factory to elect representatives to share in management control. This experiment, however, soon disappointed the hopes entertained for it, mainly because of the stubborn resistance of employers. The attempt to establish an economic parliament (*Reichswirtschaftsrat*), with equal representation for employers and workers proved similarly disappointing. The economy was soon in an economic recession and then a depression by 1922 which paved the way for the rise of Hitler and the Third Reich of the Nazi Party.

In 1929, the start of the world economic depression following the crash of the United States stock market in October 1929 gave Hitler a chance. As unemployment skyrocketed in Germany, voters turned against parties associated with the Weimar Republic. The Nazis score a series of successes in state elections. Hitler benefits from the deep divisions among the other German political parties.

The Communists hope to profit from the Depression. They blame Germany's problems on capitalism, call for a revolution, and refuse to cooperate with any of the other parties. Conservative nationalist parties blame parliamentary democracy and the Versailles treaty for Germany's problems. They hope to use the economic crisis to overturn the constitution and restore an authoritarian system similar to the pre-war monarchy. They see Hitler as a potentially helpful ally. The Social Democratic Party is the most vigorous defender of the democratic system but blames the "bourgeois" pro-capitalist parties for the economic crisis. The Catholic Center party has the most significant weight in the government but has no remedy for the Depression. By contrast, the Nazis offer a simple explanation of the crisis—it's the fault of the Jews—and a simple program for ending it. In national parliamentary elections in September 1930, the Nazis scored an unexpected success, winning 18% of the vote and becoming the second-largest party (after the Social Democrats). In early 1932, the unpopular coalition government of the Centre Party failed to gain support and a new party elections election in July, where Hitler ran for president against the celebrated war hero Hindenburg and won 37% of the votes of democracy in Germany, whilst the Communists got 16%.

No majority coalition in favour of democracy can be established any more. Various politicians compete with each other to create a government that will rule by decree. Hitler was offered a place in one of these schemes, engineered by Kurt Von Schleicher, in August 1932, but refused because he would not have complete control. Ne elections are held in November to break the deadlock. For the first time since 1929, the Nazis' share of the vote goes down to 32%. Fearing that his moment may be about to pass Hitler becomes more conciliatory to Von Schleicher; on January 30, 1933, an agreement was announced. Hitler was named Chancellor (prime minister). Despite the broad support for the Nazis, the party had only four seats in the cabinet. Von Schleicher and other conservatives expect Hitler's extremism to undermine his popularity; they will then be able to dismiss him and keep power themselves. It was the Great Depression that created the conditions in which Hitler could come to power; although his party did become the largest in Germany, Hitler was not elected to office; the Nazis never won an absolute majority of votes, even in the final elections held after they came to power in March 1933; Hitler became Chancellor thanks to the calculations of right-wing nationalist politicians who thought they could use his popularity to destroy the Weimar system. Hitler, of course, had other ideas once he gained control.

Adolf Hitler was completely wrong about absolutely everything...usually. When Hitler said something correctly, it was merely to set up the next lie. As with all good propagandists—and he certainly was that—he would begin with a few obvious, documented facts and then distort them horribly. At any rate, the infamous German Führer's worm-tongue rhetoric is 'not' to be taken seriously except as a classic example of the sort of masterful demagoguery from which appropriate lessons may hopefully be learned. Here is an extract from his speech to the German Hitler youth in September 1935. Already, he has a master plan to eventually use them in war as reserve forces for front-line fighting that ultimately resulted in the loss of many thousands of their lives.

"German Youth! For the third time, you have assembled over 50,000 representatives of a community growing larger yearly for this parade. The importance of those you represent here each year has constantly increased. Not just in terms of numbers; no, we see it here in terms of value. When I think back to our first and second parades and compare today's parade with those, I see the same development we can see in all other aspects of German national life today. Our People are becoming visibly more disciplined, fit and trim, and our youth is beginning to follow this lead. The idea of what a man should be has not always been the same, even among our People. There were times - they seem to be long ago, and we can scarcely understand them - when the ideal young German was the young fellow who could handle his beer and liquor. Today, I can say with joy that we no longer idealise the young fellow who can handle his beer and liquor but the young man who can face any weather, the tough young man. What matters is not merely how many glasses of beer he can drink but how many blows he can withstand, not how many nights he can spend doing the rounds of the bars and pubs but how many kilometres he can march. Today, the German People's ideal is no longer your average beer drinker but the young men and girls who are fit and trim."

In September 1935, he gave a short speech at Nuremberg: " Nothing is possible unless none will commands, a will which has to be obeyed by others, beginning at the top and ending at the bottom. This is the expression of an authoritarian state of a weak, babbling democracy. Everyone is proud to obey in this authoritarian state because he knows: I will likewise be obeyed when I take command."

To justify the annexation of Austria on 8th April 1938, Hitler called a public vote on whether the unification of Austria and Germany would stand. This is an excerpt from his speech the day before the vote. "When one day we shall be no more than the coming generation shall be able to look back with pride upon this day, the day in which a great Volk affirmed the German community. In the past, millions of German men shed their blood for this Reich. How merciful a fate to be allowed to create this Reich today without suffering. Now, rise. Subscribe to German Volk, and hold it tightly in your hands! I wish to thank Him who allowed me to return to my homeland so that I could return it to my German Reich! May every German realise the importance of the hour tomorrow. Assess and then bow his head in reverence before the will of the Almighty, who has wrought this miracle on us within these past few weeks." Hitler took Austria without shedding blood, but it was not so when he took Poland. Just the week before the launching of the attack on Poland, Hitler made an address to the Chief Commanders at Chersalzberg on 22 August 1939.

"Our strength consists in our speed and our brutality. Genghis Khan led millions of women and children to slaughter – with premeditation and a happy heart. History sees in him solely the founder of a state. It's a matter of indifference to me what a weak Western European civilisation will say about me. I have issued the command – and I'll have anybody who utters but one word of criticism executed by a firing squad – that our aim does not consist in reaching certain lines but in the physical destruction of the enemy. Accordingly, I have placed my death-head formation in readiness – for the present only in the East – with orders to them to send to death mercilessly and without compassion men, women, and children of Polish derivation and language. Only thus shall we gain the living space which we need. Who, after all, speaks today of the annihilation of the Armenians?'

Hitler, in April 1945, wrote to his command his last order to read to the soldiers on the German Eastern Front; it was his previous lie. He had almost deceived himself in believing: "The Jewish Bolshevik arch-enemy has gone over to the attack with his masses for the last time. He attempts to smash Germany and eradicate our nation. You soldiers from the east today already know yourselves to a large extent what fate is threatening, above all, German women, girls and children. While old men and children are being murdered, women and girls are humiliated to the status of barracks prostitutes. Others are marched off to Siberia. We have anticipated this thrust, and since January of this year, everything has been done to build a strong front. Mighty artillery is meeting the enemy. Countless new units replenished our infantry's casualties. Reserve units, new formations and the Volkssturm reinforce our front. This time, the Bolsheviks will experience Asia's old fate. That is, he must and will bleed to death in front of the capital of the German Reich.

Whosoever does not do his duty now is a traitor to our nation. The regiment or division that leaves its position acts so disgracefully that it will have to be ashamed before the women and children who are withstanding the bombing terror in our towns. Above all, look out for the treacherous few officers and soldiers who, to secure their own miserable lives, will fight against us in Russian pay, perhaps even in German uniform. Unless you know him well, whoever gives you a command to retreat will be arrested immediately and, if necessary, executed immediately, irrespective of rank.

Suppose every soldier on the Eastern Front fulfils his duty in these coming days and weeks. In that case, Asia's last onslaught will collapse just as in the end, our enemies' penetration in the West will, despite everything, come to naught. Berlin remains German, Vienna will again be German, and Europe will never be Russian. From one community, you are sworn to defend not a vain conception of fatherland but to defend your homeland, women, children and thus your future. In this hour, the entire German nation looks to you, my soldiers in the east, and only hopes that your fanaticism, bye your arms and your leadership, the Bolshevik onslaught is drowned in a blood bath. At the moment when fate has taken the most significant war criminal of all time from this earth, the war will take a decisive turn."

(Signed) ADOLF HITLER

In the final hours of the war, Hitler's propaganda machine was still in modus operandi despite many of his commanders and troops surrendering to the Allies. Many of the German people receiving word of the atrocities of the concentration camps believed Hitler was unaware of what was happening; they, to the last month of the war, believed Hitler's lies.

Even today, people speak of the might of the Nazi machine and the turning of the economy around before, during and after the economic depression of the 1930s. Whilst some speak with pride of Nazi achievements; the Autobahn road network that runs through the heart of Germany, the brilliance of the well-oiled train network that is still second to none. They, too, looked with the pride of the nation when Hitler committed to providing families with a cheap German-made car. The Volkswagen- the people's car, founded in 1937 by the German labour front under the Nazi Party and revived into a global brand as it is known today post World War 11; it is known from the ironic Beetle and serves as the flagship of the Volkswagen Group, the largest automotive manufacturer by world standards. These outstanding achievements fall under the shadow of the death of millions whose blood washes away any grand notion of what was achieved under Adolf Hitler and the Third Reich.

Long before Adolf Hitler died in the Bunker, Alois Heidler acknowledged his son Adolf, which was considered to legitimise him. The mother, whose surname was Schicklgurber, bore a son out of wedlock to a man named Heidler (pronounced Hitler). Herr Heidler, being Adolf, changed his name to his father's name but spelled it Hitler.

And now for the fiction mixed with fact. Only a small group of officials and Eva Bruen knew that Hitler himself had a son. Hitler had arranged for his son to leave the country with a passport and a letter of introduction to the Catholic church authorities in Rome who were helping Nazies escape at the war's end. The son had fled as a refugee with a Nazi female sympathiser and made their way to Rome, where reportedly Adolf Hitler's grandson was born. There is no proof of a grandson but fiction would have it that He was named Alois Shicklgurber.

It is supposed that Alois Shicklgruber took his paternal great-grandmother's name, Shicklgruber and his great-grandfather's Christian name, Alois, obtained a certificate upon registering his birth at the Vatican official office in Rome before being baptised into the Catholic faith. Hitler's son and his partner died under mysterious circumstances in Rome. The news of the day would have it that their son found in his father's meagre possessions a letter that reported he was Adolf Hitler's grandson. So it was that Alois was adopted by a Jesuit priest and educated into far-right totalitarian socio-political ideology and saturated with the symbolism and signs of Christian theology.

This mentor priest was something of a radical thinker, but deep down a Nazi sympathiser, for he instilled into the young man the sufferings and death of Christ for sinful man come about by the hatred of the Jewish rabies for a rebel preacher. In Christian theology, Jesus is the Lamb provided by God himself as the sacrifice for the wrongdoings of mankind . Catholics believe that it is this same body, sacrificed on the cross and risen on the third day and united with Christ's divinity, soul and blood which is made present in the offering of each Eucharistic sacrifice. It was Hitler's warped thinking that burnt offerings of Jews in the concentration camps were sacred and it may be assumed for the sake of the story that it was the view of t of his acolyte Alois Shicklgurber

By the time Alois Shicklgurber reached manhood, he had not only studied for the priesthood and gained a doctorate in theology at Rome University, but he had also formulated a secret society participating in occult practices bent on renewing a commitment to the passions and mission of his great grandfather Adolf Hitler.

CHAPTER 3.

THE RISE OF A FOURTH REICH

In the bowels of the Vatican, underground is a cemetery, "the city of the dead," an extensive and elaborate burial place of an ancient city. It was initially the location of the "Circus of Caligula," a chariot-racing enthusiast who began constructing a circus, which was completed in the time of Claudius in 45 -54 AD. The circus was also the palace of St. Peter and St. Paul's martyrdom. The circus was abandoned by the middle of the second century AD when the area was partitioned and given in concession to private individuals to construct tombs in the cemetery. The Old St. Peters Basilica was erected by Constantine over the site using some of the existing structures of the Circus of Nero. The basilica was sited so that its' domed roof contained an altar, and far above it is the tomb of St. Peter in the current day St. Peter's Basilica. Most of the ruins of the Circus survived until 1450 when they were finally destroyed by the construction of the new St. Peter's Basilica. A stairwell some 12 metres deep lies below the burial place of St Peter and many Popes and Saints. Along a corridor at this level between ancient ruins is a locked hidden chapel except for those who have access to it when a Black Mass for the dead is performed there.

This was the place that Alios Shicklgurber discovered in his visits to the Basilica catacombs and where he was to band together a group of like-minded priests and Nazi sympathisers to hold regular meetings combining the symbols of the ancient Roman Empire, the Third Reich and performed a weekly Black Mass of the Last Supper. It was his dark broader strategy of a new regime of a Reich to shape public opinion and reconquer the world on the back of the mission of the Third Reich in the vain hope of the glory of Lucifer, the defected nature of the Godhead to whom those who followed had come to acknowledge as their guiding light on earth for the growth of a new world order.

Reverend Father Alios Shicklgurber, Jesuit priest, teacher, theologian, and founder of an occult bent on the glorification of his grandfather, to renew Hitler's mission. That of a toxic blend of racism, anti-semitism, occult symbolism and black magic rituals reenacted towards a one-world order in the shape of a fourth Reich. He, of all spiritual leaders, understood the capacity to reason as an individual and, collectively, to let go of the desires that ultimately lead to living in the dark and slowly but surely be enlightened to both the evil within us and the world's evil. He reportedly promoted the notion that the choice is always ours, to follow the dictates of the Golden Rule of the heart by living in accord with loving God-like principles for our betterment or continue to be possessed by our basic instincts, which will ultimately lead us to death and destruction. Death and destruction at the hands of the Anti-Christ. This was his outward persona in sermons he preached to the faithful within the bounds of Catholic teaching. However, privately, he had long since given up the faith in favour of hidden occult goals.

Alois and his associate occult members had a mission to become the foundation fathers of a new Fourth Reich; like Hitler, borrowing symbols from this powerful historical Roman entity, they also sought to associate themselves with strength, power, and authority. They realised the weakness in the Christian authorities and Jewish-funded one-world governments. Again, like the Nazies, they associated themselves with this historical era of the Roman Empire; they aimed to portray themselves as inheritors of a great and advanced civilisation. They saw themselves as a new global empire and sought to draw parallels between the ambitions of Hitler's Nazi regime and those of the Ancient Romans, known for their conquests and expansion. Rome had lots of imagery that almost everyone in Europe and the US has copied. Kaiser is German for Caesar; Tzar is Russian for Caesar, and Nazi Germany adopted the symbols of Rome (even though Italy, Rome, was fascist at that point and had a much better claim on being the rightful owners) and pagan Europe.

So, this supposed leader of the forces of darkness, Reverent Olios Schicklgurber, cleverly utilised the symbolism of the Roman Empire and Roman Catholic Church teachings by dabbling in the occult practices of black masses as an offering to his shadow Christ figure Lucifer, the Morning Star who had, in his opinion, been wrongly cast down by God for his disobedience at the beginning of creation. Father Olios also had a warped view that not only did Jesus Christ, the light of lights, be crucified on the Cross as a sacrificial act for the salvation of mankind, but the other son, Lucifer, who was the Prince of the Darkness, had been overlooked and had died on that cross in a spiritual sense in what he considered was Christ's darker side that never was displayed by him on his mission of salvation for mankind. whilst on earth. Father Schucklgurber had a notion that a sacrificial act of a Black Mass on Good Friday would make his mission of a Fourth Reich legitimised in the eyes of Lucifer. A Sacrificial act of a mocked offering in an occult ceremony would legitimise the death and resurrection of the angel of death, and a new world order would soon transpire.

So it was that the young priest was enraged with the Hitler-like militaristic ambitions of Nazism that had plunged the world into chaos in WW11 and brought about the death of millions as a consequence devised his plan. It was not dissimilar to Hitler's ability to rally support behind his vision of a Reich. Through his planned, charismatic speeches, he planned to restore a body of a symbolic but warped spiritual elitism of greatness to captivate the hearts and minds of many in today's world who were desperate for a better future.

This priest now believed he would be able to manipulate and sway those who belonged to his occult network of religious extremists and a body of Elite opportunists, intellectual genesis, and programmed assassins who would significantly influence his rise to power and ultimately establish a Fourth Reich to overtake world power. His fanaticism had overridden his soul search for God's light and guidance to allow his character defects to take the upper hand in his decision-making. The scales of justice weighed heavily on the dark side for him and, for that, his followers. He had mistakenly used the dictates of Nazi history and his theological learning to unwittingly unleash evil intent, where before his occultism his intended soul searching had been honourable. The priest's acute intellect hid this in his occasional oratory, had all the rantings and rage of his grandfather, Adolf Hitler.

The wayward priest also believed in Hitler's warped belief in his Catholic faith, blaming the Jews for crucifying Christ and controlling him. Hitler, of course, also blamed the Jewish control of the money flow, which resulted in the financial difficulties and unemployment of post-war Germany, and his unemployment difficulties before joining the army. [The origin of Hitler's hatred of Jews is not clear. In *Mein Kampf*, he described his development into an antisemite as the result of a long, personal struggle. Supposedly, his aversion to everything Jewish came to fruition when he lived and worked as a painter in Vienna (1908-1913). One way or another, it is clear that Hitler came into contact with antisemitic ideas at an early age. *

Father Olios had a historical viewpoint of the hatred of Jews. He knew that Hitler did not invent the hatred of Jews. Jews in Europe had been victims of discrimination and persecution since the Middle Ages, often for religious reasons. Christians saw the Jewish faith as an aberration that had to be quashed. Jews were sometimes forced to convert, or they were not allowed to practise certain professions. In the nineteenth century, religion played a less critical role. It was replaced by theories about the differences between races and peoples. The idea that Jews belonged to a different people than the Germans, for instance, caught on. Even Jews who had converted to Christianity were still 'different' because of their bloodline.

So, on a particular Easter Sunday, a story was later told that Father Olios Schicklgurber made his way down the dark stairwell corridor to the hidden chapel in the catacombs, where twelve of his disciples had begun dark rituals. He opened the heavy wooden door at the back of the altar with a key that he alone had in his possession. The ritual black mass was in the process of reenacting the last supper of Jesus when he entered. He stood centre stage and took over the proceedings surrounded by twelve of his fellow occult members whose bodies and faces were cloaked by a long black robe with the symbol of the swastika embroidered on their chest plate.

The priest had become obsessed with the symbolism of a blood sacrifice of a small lamb as an offering to his appointed Godhead; the one whose destiny had always been centred on death. One of the local members had been given a gift of a lamb for the sacrificial service. As the lamb was slayed on the altar its final bleeding was soon stopped as Father Olios pierced the animal's heart with a knife killing it instantaneously. The priest then held a silver cup over the lamb's body and drained blood into it from the flesh wound near the heart, drinking some of the contents; "This is the blood of Christ" he cried out before passing his 'cup of eternal salvation' around to the robed twelve apostles of the dark side to drink of the cup of this sacrificial act. They each prayed as one to Lucifer to bless and influence their actions for humanity. The occult apostles took the heart out of the lamb and each in turn ate of the flesh saying: "This is the body of Lucifer Christ in whom we are guided." The remainder of the lamb was burnt in an urn over the altar and an essence of smoke arose as they prayed in homage to their misguided belief that good intent would follow from their actions. Then taking the urn of ashes they sat it in front of the Skull and Bones symbol beneath a bust of Hitler strategically placed nearby.

So it was Easter Monday evening, the night after the sacrificing of the lamb at Black Mass the previous day, that Father Olios and his evil cronies gathered together, with many of his followers of a misguided belief, in an amphitheatre on the outskirts of Rome, to devise and implement his racist, exclusionary, anti-democratic, aggressive, intolerant movement along similar central tenets of National Socialism that Hitler's Third Reich had as their mission. Hitler's came about through propaganda, death and destruction of human values and human beings. The priest was mindful of the failure of his grandfather's ultimate plan, but he had no immediate plans to wipe out the race of Jewish leaders but rather to infiltrate all areas of world leadership and change them from within.

As he mounted the stage and stood before a bank of microphones, the priest gazed out across the large crowd and looked skyward. It had turned blood red and he was reminded of the revelation to Sister Lucy of Fatima fame when she related in her third memoir in August 1941: " God made use of this to make me understand His justice was about to strike the guilty nations.." Of course, this radicalised priest now saw this as a sign of the beginning of his campaign and not the beginning of another world War in which dire predictions were revealed in the second secret at Fatima.

Hitler had declared upon seeing the red sky on 25th January 1938 "Now there will be blood," and decided to invade Poland which was the beginning of the war, although a state of war had not been 'officially' declared by major world powers against one another at the time, a state of war did exist and it was in the time Pius X1 was still in the Vatican as Pontiff. The Virgin Mary back there in Portugal in 1917 had prophesied: ". crimes, using war, famine, and persecutions of the Church and the Holy Father...' Within two months of the great sign, Hitler's armies invaded Austria on the 9th March 1938 and the annexation of Czechoslovakia, the formation of a military alliance without firing one shot. This too was as the Blessed Virgin had prophesied, the Second World War began 'in the reign of Pius XI',"

During the night of January 25-26, 1938, in Moscow's Lubianka prison, a man by the name of Kristian Rakovsky had announced that 'the great sign given by God that He is about to punish the world' was being interrogated by Josef Stalin's chief interrogator. During the interrogation, Rakovsky revealed Germany's plan to dominate Europe. He proposed that the Soviet Union join Germany in an invasion of Poland, which would lead to Europe's retaliation against Germany and not the Soviet Union. According to Rakovsky's plan, France and England would wear each other out, after which the Soviet Union would turn on Germany and collect the spoils of the war. This fateful interview began at the same time the unknown light in the sky was beginning to fade. It resulted in the Soviet Union's instigation of and participation in the war, and Rakovsky's plan was carried out to the great benefit of the Soviet Union. Again, this decisive step toward World War II occurred during the reign of Pope Pius XI.

It was his predecessor who struck so much controversy with the Church and the Allies after WW11. Few topics in Church history, or the history of the Second World War, are as hotly contested as Pius XII's decision to avoid direct public criticism of Hitler or his regime, and to remain publicly silent in the face of the Holocaust. Many Church conservatives portray Pius as nonetheless a steadfast, courageous foe of Hitler and fascism. Others have harshly criticised him for failing to denounce the Nazi war of aggression and Hitler's effort to exterminate all of Europe's Jews. Even when the Nazi SS rounded up more than 1,000 Jews in Rome itself, on October 16, 1943, the pope refused to make his voice heard. Held for two days in a complex near the walls of the Vatican, the Jews were then placed on a train bound for Auschwitz.

Father Olios began his oratory:" See here," pointing to the sky. "This is the same blood-red sky given to my grandfather Adolf Hitler whose aims and ambitions were for the unity of the Arian race, the peoples of Germany of his time who had suffered great hardships by the influences of the wealth who robed from the poor to give to the rich. His aims were pure and his methodology swift. The plan only failed because he was to depend upon foreign capital to fund the war which would have been beneficial to all by eradicating the Jewish influence of his time who controlled world finance." This was partly true, but in the main, it was built on a lie. The priest knew it not to be so. Like Hitler, he blamed the money Elites, and Masonic members of the banking sector for Hitler's ultimate lack of funds and supplies to carry the war to his Socialistic conclusions. But as one learns in time, the money men always play both sides for the outcome in their ultimate best interest. The priest was determined not to let this happen again, and he knew he needed to get alongside industry, governments and the international banking sector to ensure he could get his plan to work. He saw his intention as honourable and no doubt Hitler did also.

His speech laid out a plan of the world divided into twelve sectors, with twelve of his apostles overseeing the implementation of a radical plan of control. He kept the details brief, intent on gaining control of government, countries and money supply by stealth and using the International Bank of Settlements to create a One World Order in his template of a Fourth Reich. His intention was not for war, but an Armageddon of sorts would ultimately erupt if his method were ever implemented. He knew that once his coup was underway success would be driven by his coup-makers' ability to get elites and the public to believe that their coup attempt would succeed. The radical priest had a plan for the world and he knew it may well cause a total upheaval of the world we know, but he saw it as essential to implement a Fourth Reich with a template of control that differed only in its management controls to that of Hitlers Third Reich.

CHAPTER 4.

ENDLESS SHADES OF GREY

Whilst the radical priest's intent was not to shed blood, he saw it as to some degree being inevitable as Hitler had in authorising the extermination of the Jews. He knew he had to convince the International Bank of Settlements to finance his vision for a Fourth Reich. The heads of the banking, who had formally approved monies for Hitler to finance the invasion of Poland, knew that his ultimate plan was mass extermination of the Jewish race in Europe. One wonders at the extent some will go to kill their own. Perhaps the financial strength of the Jewish race was too competitive for the money makers, but one may never know other than the statement that at its heart " money is the root of all evil."

Adolf Hitler became the vice-chancellor of Germany around the 1930s but the seeds to finance the war were sowed by him much before he ascended into power. During the 1920's 30's, the German automobile market was very lucrative and General Motors as well as Ford wanted a big piece of this market to do business. As time went by, both these companies established factories in Germany which churned out automobiles for Nazi Germany. Adolf Hitler was an ardent admirer of the - American Assembly Line - style of production. He once famously remarked -"I regard Henry Ford as my inspiration." Ford too was a great admirer of Hitler's dictatorial style of governing. They communicated regularly and Ford sent Hitler a cheque for USD 50,000 every year on his birthday. It was no doubt a ploy to keep the erratic Hitler onside so Ford would gain more contracts for his engines which were being built for the running of water pumps on farms, tractors, cars and ultimately tank engines.

The ingenuity of Ford was the fact that the engine blocks for all the various uses were interchangeable with any machine. It was however the German's own Volkswagen group that got the ultimate contract for the building of a people's car commissioned by Hitler in the better times of finance by the International banking sector. Ford didn't miss out despite this, and Hitler sent two of his officers to America before the USA entered the Second World War, Henry Ford was awarded the Iron Cross for his contribution to Germany's mechanisation; much to the disgust of many of his fellow countrymen.

Whilst monies to run the country and the war were funded under the approval of the International Bank of Settlements, the **German** government funded much of its military effort through plunder, especially plundering the wealth of Jewish citizens and the like.

However, after Hitler invaded Czechoslovakia, another sinister plot was put into play when, just six months before Britain went to war with Nazi Germany, the Bank of England willingly handed over 5.6 million pounds worth of gold to Hitler and it belonged to Czechoslovakia. It was not just with the infamous Munich agreement of September 1938, which allowed the Nazis to annex the Sudetenland, but also in London, where Montagu Norman, the eccentric but ruthless governor of the Bank of England, agreed to surrender gold owned by the National Bank of Czechoslovakia. The Czechoslovak gold was held in London in a sub-account in the name of the Bank for International Settlements, the Basel-based bank for central banks. When the Nazis marched into Prague in March 1938, they immediately sent armed soldiers to the offices of the National Bank.

The Czech directors were ordered, on pain of death, to send two transfer requests. The first instructed the Bank of International Settlements to transfer 23.1 metric tonnes of gold from the Czechoslovak BIS account held at the Bank of England to the Reichsbank BIS account held at Threadneedle Street.

The second order instructed the Bank of England to transfer almost 27 metric tonnes of gold held in the National Bank of Czechoslovakia's name to the BIS's gold account at the Bank of England. To outsiders, the distinction between the accounts seems obscure. Yet it proved crucial - and allowed Norman to ensure that the first order was carried out. The Czechoslovak bank officials believed that as the orders had been carried out under duress, neither would be allowed to go through. But they had not reckoned on the bureaucrats running the BIS and the determination of Montague Norman to see that procedures were followed, even as his country prepared for war with Nazi Germany. His decision caused uproar, both in the press and in Parliament.

George Strauss, a Labour MP, spoke for many when he thundered in Parliament:"The Bank for International Settlements is the bank which sanctions the most notorious outrage of this generation the rape of Czechoslovakia." Winston Churchill demanded to know how the government could ask its citizens to enlist in the military when it was "so butter-fingered that pounds 6 million worth of gold can be transferred to the Nazi government." It was a good question. Thanks to Norman and the BIS, Nazi Germany had just looted 23.1 tonnes of gold without a shot being fired. The second transfer order for the gold held in the National Bank of Czechoslovakia's name did not go through. Sir John Simon, the Chancellor of the Exchequer, had instructed banks to block all Czechoslovak assets.*

The documents the Bank of England released reveal what they show and omit. They are a window into a world of fearful deference to authority, the primacy of procedure over morality, a world where, for the bankers, the most important thing is to keep the channels of international finance open, no matter what the human cost—a world, in other words, not entirely different from today.

The Bank of International Settlements is a unique hybrid: a commercial bank protected by an international treaty. Its assets can never be seized, even in times of war, and it pays no taxes on profits. The Czechoslovaks believed that the BIS's legal immunities would protect them. But they were wrong.

The Bank of England's historian argued that to refuse the transfer order would have been a breach of Britain's treaty obligations about the BIS. There was a powerful counter-argument that the Nazi invasion of Czechoslovakia had rendered any such obligations null and void as the country no longer existed. A key sentence in the Bank of England documents is on page 1,295. It reads: "The general attitude of the Bank of England directors of the BIS during the war was governed by their anxiety to keep the BIS to play its part in the solution of post-war problems". The secret history of the BIS and its strong relationship with the Bank of England becomes ever more murky.

During the war, the BIS proclaimed that it was neutral, a view supported by the Bank of England. The BIS was so entwined with the Nazi economy that it helped keep the Third Reich in business. It carried out foreign exchange deals for the Reichsbank bank; it accepted looted Nazi gold; it recognised the puppet regimes installed in occupied countries, which, together with the Third Reich, soon controlled the majority of the bank's shares. Indeed, the BIS was so helpful for the Nazis that Emil Puhl, the vice-president of the Reichsbank bank and BIS director, referred to the BIS as the Reichsbank's only "foreign branch".

The BIS's reach and connections were vital for Germany. So much so that all through the war, the Reichsbank continued paying interest on the monies lent by the BIS. The BIS used this interest to pay dividends to shareholders, including the Bank of England. Thus, the Reichsbank funded the British war economy through the BIS. After the war, five BIS directors were tried for war crimes, including Schacht. "They don't hang bankers," Schacht supposedly said, and he was right he was acquitted.

Buried among the typewritten pages of the Bank of England's history is a name of whom few have ever heard, a man for whom, like Montague Norman, the priority of international finance reigned over mere national considerations. Thomas McKittrick, an American banker, was president of the BIS. When the United States entered the war in December 1941, McKittrick's position, the history notes, "became difficult". But McKittrick managed to keep the bank in business, thanks partly to his friend Allen Dulles, the US spymaster based in Berne. McKittrick was an asset of Dulles, known as Codename 644, and frequently passed him information that he had garnered from Emil Puhl, a frequent visitor to Basel and often met McKittrick.

Declassified documents in the American intelligence archives reveal an even more disturbing story. Under an intelligence operation known as the "Harvard Plan", McKittrick was in contact with Nazi industrialists, working towards what the US documents, dated February 1945, described as a "close cooperation between the Allied and German business world." Thus, while Allied soldiers were fighting through Europe, McKittrick was cutting deals to keep the German economy strong. This happened with what the US documents describe as "the full assistance" of the State Department.

Bank of England history also disparaged Harry Dexter White, an official in the Treasury Department Bank history notes who rather sneeringly, had said of the BIS: "There is an American president doing business with the Germans while our boys are fighting the Germans."

Aided by its powerful friends, such as Montague Norman, Allen Dulles and much of Wall Street, the BIS survived the attempts by Norman and White to close it down. The bank's allies used precisely the argument detailed on page 1,295 of the Bank of England's history: the BIS was needed to plan the post-war European economy. From the 1950s to the 1990s, the BIS hosted much of the planning and technical preparation for introducing the euro. Without the BIS, the euro would not exist.

The BIS remains very profitable. Although it has only about 140 customers (it refuses to say how many), it made a tax-free profit of about 900 million pounds last year. Every other month, it hosts the Global Economy Meetings, where 60 of the most powerful central bankers, including Mark Carney, Governor of the Bank of England, meet. No details of meetings are released, even though the attendees are public servants charged with managing national economies.

Looking back on the loans approved by the BIS for the Nazi mission of war without any security from Germany, and at the expense of Czechoslovakia gold as a security one wonders about the sanity of the lenders. However, it is possible Hitler's plan for the domination of Europe, eliminating the potential threat from France, securing economic resources of Western Europe, and forcing the UK to come to terms seemed to work in the interest of the BIS at the time. His mission was to conquer Eastern Europe and its racial reordering to create a European version of the American West, with Germans as settlers, and the indigenous population enslaved and eventually eliminated. This would provide a launching pad for rivalry with the UK and USA for world domination. A plan akin to the Jewish banker Elite's earlier mission for a One World Order sat well with them.

Things had not worked out too well for the International bankers after WW1. A new era of German political prosperity was foreseen after the end of that war when in November 1918 Kaiser Wilhelm 11, who had ruled the country for 30 years had abdicated, the monarchy was abolished and a new republic was to be formed in its stead. The authoritarian style of rule that had characterised Germany since the unification of the nation in 1871 was to be replaced by a parliamentary democracy. This Weimar Republic subsequently drafted one of the most advanced liberal constitutions in Europe at the time, with clauses guaranteeing freedom of speech, assembly of worship, universal suffrage and unfettered elections. Just fifteen years later, all of this lay in tatters as Adolf Hitler stripped away people's civil rights and imposed his brutal dictatorial governance.

The fledgling Weimar Republic faced tremendous social, economic and political challenges from the word go. There was a failure to enact a social revolution in 1918-19. There was growing public unrest about the state of the German war effort. This erupted in a sailors mutiny in a key seaport followed by the formation of workers and soldiers councils across Germany, which, inspired by the success of the Russian Revolution a year earlier, demanded a complete political change. Whilst German manufacturing boomed in the Roaring Twenties, all came to an economic collapse long before the devastating impact of the 1929 Stock market collapse followed by the Great Depression, which, at its peak left six million Germans unemployed. Such difficulties highlighted the government's slow response to the crisis, its inability to cope with the sudden surge in welfare demands, and the aptitude of extreme groups like Hitler's Nazi party and its propaganda. Even more significant in the 1930s many Weimar politicians were simply unwilling to take measures to safeguard the fragile democracy.

Whilst on paper the Weimar Republic made a pact with Army officials to enable the old elite to be left in place; this meant no interference nor any radical restructuring of German society transpired. These people would simply bide their time and wait for an opportunity to regain the initiative and restore Germany to its former way of life. There was fear from the political right of Bolshevism, whilst members of the political left had realised that reform would remain limited with this Republic.

A series of weak coalition governments fragmented the political system, hindering the passage of legislation and enabling extremist parties to gain a great voice in the Reichstag during these times of popular unrest. Even more significant was the fact that the Weimar Republic was weakened by the economic legacy of the First World War. Even before the Treaty of Versailles had thrown reparation payments into the mix, the Germans were contending with vast amounts of debt and spiralling inflation. The nail in the coffin was the exacerbated infamous 1919 peace treaty. Germany was compelled to pay billions of compensation to the Allies while at the same time being stripped of some of her most industrial-rich territories.

By 1923 the country was in the grip of hyperinflation, the currency was worthless and millions of people had lost their life savings. Whilst the introduction of a new currency, the Rentenmark, enabled the economy to recover somewhat, the shadow of reparations continued to loom over the rest of the interwar period. Two international agreements, The Dawes Plan of 1925, and the Young Plan of 1929 would revise the overall amount Germany had to pay, and enable her to borrow the necessary funds from the United States which already had vast interests in German industrialisation and agriculture. The economic burdens imposed after WWI remained extremely unpopular, providing powerful ammunition to right-wing groups who called for a complete rejection of the Versailles settlement. The reliance on US loans also left Germany especially vulnerable to further disaster when the Wall Street Crash struck in October 1929.

The new republic simply lacked popular legitimacy, parliamentary democracy was still a novelty in Germany at the time and was viewed with suspicion. Many took on the viewpoint that they were "republican by reason"- and would go ahead with the new system whilst there were any other alternate options but they were not wholly convinced considering the Republic had no rational nor strategic decision making. It was considered by many as a dressed-up petty drama lacking any go-ahead. It begs the question that if the Republicans didn't capture the hearts and minds of the public at its beginning would they be prepared to fight for it when under attack by the opposition?

The more significant contribution to the failure of the Republic was its unfortunate association with Germany's recent defeat in WW1 and the subsequent Armistice signed by politicians. That the same men were Jewish added further to the ' stab in the back' rhetoric being peddled by right-wing political activists. This combined with the fledging government being forced to sign the Treaty of Versailles ensured the view that the Republic was tainted from the very start. It was not just the Nazis who spent the next few years campaigning for a reversal of the agreement but the majority of great Germany too.

Ultimately, the Weimar Republic has been recognised as a postwar society struggling to make the transition to peace after a bloody four-year conflict that had left the nation psychologically scarred, demographically depleted and economically weakened, The violence of street riots, classes with paramilitary groups and bloody skirmishes of political enemies with contra opinions, as to well as the popular militarism and aggressive nationalism persisted into a border popular culture of continuing to war as a glorious and noble pursuit. The younger males considered they had missed out, and many joined the Hitler Youth which became an important outlet for their expression.

The Weimar Republic narrative of Germany was doomed to fail. The notion that a Hitler-type figure was somehow inevitable was too simplistic and failed to take into account the political choices that were available to Germany in the 1920s and 1930s. In the 1920s it was the golden years and looked like the Republic might survive. Germany entered the stage of a vibrant international " League of Nations" becoming a member of what seemed to be a culture of vibrant flourishing modernity.

It was an era of new technologies, and rising consumer culture particularly driven by the USA, and in Germany, significant welfare reforms were put in -play which helped to justify a more positive assessment of the republic- yet there was no silence in the reactionary voices of the majority. The perceived loss of traditional family values, the women's movement which broke with gender norms and joined the workforce, Others demeaned the Americanisation of Germany, and a flight from the land to the cities, especially youth looking for opportunities did not help matters. In short, there was no single factor that could be held up to explain the collapse of the Weimar Republic in 1933. Political disappointment, economic crisis, social stress and a general lack of passion for a democracy combined to create a perfect storm that Hitler and the Nazis took advantage of. Hitler without any convictions of a plan to rebuild Germany seized power and with the aid of BIS funds and US further financial loans began his campaign to take over Europe with a mission of One World domination by the Nazies Third Reich under his leadership.

Intense public desire for charismatic leaders offers fertile ground for the use of propaganda. Through a carefully orchestrated public image of Nazi Party leader Adolf Hitler, during the politically unstable Weimar period the Nazis exploited this yearning to consolidate power and foster national unity.

Nazi propaganda facilitated the rapid rise of the Nazi Party to a position of political prominence and, ultimately, the control of a nation by the Nazi leadership. In particular, election campaign materials from the 1920s and early 1930s, as well as compelling visual materials and vigilantly controlled public appearances, coalesced to create a " cult of the Fuhrer" around Adolf Hitler. His fame only grew via speeches he delivered at mass rallies, parades, and on the radio. In this public persona, Nazi propagandists cast Hitler as a soldier at the ready, as a father figure, and ultimately as a messianic leader brought to redeem Germany.

CHAPTER 5.

THE MEN BEHIND THE THRONE

Modern techniques of propaganda—including strong images and simple messages—helped propel the Austrian-born Hitler from a little-known extremist to a leading candidate in the 1932 German presidential elections. World War I propaganda significantly influenced the young Hitler, who served as a soldier on the front from 1914 to 1918. Like many others, Hitler firmly believed that Germany lost the war not because of defeat on the battlefield, but as a result of enemy propaganda. He surmised that the victors of World War I (Britain, France, the United States, and Italy) had pounded home clear, simple messages that encouraged their forces while sapping the German will to fight. Hitler understood the power of symbols, oratory, and image, and formulated party slogans to reach the masses that were simple, concrete, and emotionally appealing.

The Jesuit priest, the Supreme Commander of an occult Fourth Reich sat contemplating his next plan of action to work towards the destruction of Christian values as they now seem to be, to appoint leaders whose duty it would be to turn the world economies on their heads, and set in motion a militant campaign with loyal subordinates intent on take away humanities civil rights and appointing a new world of martial laws.

It was the day after the priest had given his maiden speech on the new wave of the Reich about to be implemented, he contemplating his plan of action, as he had already devised a way of breaking the world into twelve sectors which could be centrally managed from his Rome headquarters. A One World Order of control using computer networking and a secret group of international elite controlled social propaganda, bank regulations and orchestrated economic sanctions. and a world army was already in place with a UN front.

When Adolf Hitler was appointed Chancellor of Germany on January 30, 1933, thus bringing an end to German democracy. Guided by racist and authoritarian ideas, the Nazis abolished basic freedoms and sought to create a "Volk" community. In theory, a "Volk" community united all social classes and regions of Germany behind Hitler. In reality, the Third Reich quickly became a police state, where individuals were subject to arbitrary arrest and imprisonment.

Under the banner of the United Nations, he already had an agreement from the IBS bank to back him in his endeavour. For his mission he would set out central tenets of a new National Socialism, shaping the domestic and foreign policy of his Reich. To achieve his aims he would need leaders capable of action and he would write each a 'modus operandi', management by objective template to bring down government through the dismantling of democratic policies in all of the twelve sectors of his plan.

For the moment the radical priest sat looking back on Adolf Hitler, his grandfathers appointed subordinates and began to write down a brief of each Nazi leader interrelated to their personalities and skills. He would need to ' up the ante' on propaganda to whip up enthusiasm for his cause among, not only his loyal subjects but the populous at large in every first-world country irrespective of their current political persuasion. Hitler relied heavily on Joseph Goebbels to carry the message, so he began to write off the man.

Hitler had taken the view that it was not the job of the party leader to "appoint" leaders. He was more than ever convinced that the most effective officer was the one who won respect for himself as a leader through his achievements. In this regard, as the Minister for Propaganda, there was none better than Joseph Goebbels. He had joined the National Socialist German Workers' Party, in 1924 and did his utmost to create support to the ideology of Nazism. His talent for disseminating the Nazi message through catchy slogans, brightly coloured posters and powerful public speeches impressed Hitler. He carefully stages party rallies to demonstrate maximum emotional impact while orchestrating beer hall fights similar to serving to capture public attention.

Goebbels became district leader of Berlin in 1926 and founded the party newspaper, Der Angriff (The Attack), shortly afterwards. From 1933 Goebbels became the Reich Minister Minister for Propaganda controlling all courses of information in the Third Reich. He organised the torchlight parades on Hitler's appointment as Chancellor in 1933, oversaw the burning of "un-German" books and was intimately in the staging of the 1936 Berlin Olympics. Goebbels was also responsible for the development of the "Cult of the Fuhrer" around Hitler, crafting his image of a heroic leader.

In 1943 Gobbels delivered the infamous "Total War" speech, urging the German people to continue fighting, in the aftermath of the failed bombing plot of 1944. He was then appointed Plenipotentiary for Total War, responsible for doing everything possible to keep the German war machine operational. Renowned as Hitler's most loyal follower, he continued to fight till the bitter end. When Hitler committed suicide on 30th April 1945, Gobbles was unable to contemplate a future without him He and his wife Magda poisoned their six children with cyanide pills and then shot themselves.

Father Shicklgurber, mindful of the ultimate failure of his grandfather Adolf Hitler's mission and that of his loyal follower Joseph Goebbels, resolved that his campaign would not follow such a path. He had the ammunition of the World Wide Web at his disposal and an army of hackers, IT marketing and advertising promoters, and Reich believers across the world to skilfully manoeuvre as he willed. He took some notations of the best of Goebbels's propaganda methodology and Freudian manipulations, as he considered the next of Hitler's leader as a template for one of military might for leadership to fulfil his dream. For that, he began to take notes on Herman Goring.

Herman Goring was a veteran World War 1 fighter pilot who served with distinction and was considered an Ace pilot but was disillusioned that the war ended and influenced by his friend Adolf Hitler who was a decorated soldier himself. Goring joined the National Socialist Party in early 1923 and in the abortive Beer Hall Putsch of November 1923, in which Hitler tried to seize power prematurely. During the putsch, Goring was badly wounded in the groin. His arrest was ordered, but he escaped with his wife into Austria. Given morphine to deaden the pain from his wounds, he became so severely addicted that he twice underwent treatment in 1925–26 at the Languor mental hospital in Sweden. In 1927 he returned to Germany, where his contacts in German industry proved useful, and he was taken back into the party leadership. He occupied 1 of the 12 Reichstag seats that the Nazi Party won in the 1928 election. Thereafter Goring became the acknowledged party leader in the lower house, and, when the Nazis won 230 seats in the election of July 1932, he was elected president of the Reichstag.

Goring power continued to grow throughout the Third Reich. He became Commander in Chief of the Luftwaffe, the air weapon of the German defence forces in 1935 and then headed the Four Year Plan Office from 1936. He was a major player in preparing Germany for war and became famous for enriching himself from looted art taken mostly from Jewish families and taking over property during the conflict itself. Following early military successes he was promoted to Reichsmarshall, the highest military Office of the Reich, having command over all the armed forces. However, all turned pear shape after the defeat at Stalingrad in 1943, combined with the inability of the airforce to wipe out the British forces which led to the decline of Goring's political fortunes and he fell from grace.

In 1945 he attempted to regain power having been named Hitler's successor in the event of his death or inability to rule. This action was enough to cause him to be deemed a traitor. He was expelled from the Nazi Party, stripped of his offices and placed under house arrest. At the end of the war, he was arrested and became the chief defendant at the International Military Tribunal in Nuremberg. In October 1946, he was convicted of four counts of crimes against peace, conspiracy, war crimes and crimes against humanity. Goring was sentenced to death but evaded captors by biting onto a cyanide capsule the night before his execution was scheduled to take place.

Father Olois pondered for a moment how so many of Hitler's leaders committed suicide when the chips were down. He figured that as death is inevitable for all mankind, then it was a fair price to pay to have the benefit of exceptional talents whilst the going was good. Indeed, he had come to believe that it was the mission of Lucifer to bring about darkness and death upon humanity and it was his sworn duty to pit this evil outcome into play. He made a note of the strengths and weaknesses of Hermann Goring during his leadership in the Third Reich and pondered the leaders he already had plans for the One World Order to be enacted. He turned then to consider the most well-known of Hitler's infantrymen, Rudolf Hess.

Hess enlisted as an infantryman in the Imperial German Army during World War 1. He was wounded several times during the war and like Hitler was awarded the Iron Cross, 2nd Class, in 1915. Shortly before the war ended, Hess enrolled to train as an aviator, but he saw no action in that role. He left the armed forces in December 1918 with the rank of *Leutnant der Reserve*. In 1919, Hess enrolled in the University of Munich, where he studied geopolitics under Karl Haushoferr, a proponent of the concept of Lebensraum ('living space'), which became one of the pillars of Nazi ideology. Hess joined the Nazi Party on 1 July 1920 and was at Hitler's side on 8 November 1923 for the Beer Hall Putsch, the failed Nazi attempt to seize control of the government of Bavaria. While serving a prison sentence for this attempted coup, he assisted Hitler with *Mein Kampf*, which became the foundation of the political platform of the Nazi Party.

After Hitler became Chancellor in January 1933, Hess was appointed Deputy *Führer* of the Nazi Party in April. He was elected to the Reichstag in the March elections, was made a Reichsleiter of the Nazi Party in June and in December 1933 he became Minister without Portfolio in Hitler's cabinet. He was also appointed in 1938 to the Cabinet Council and in August 1939 to the Council of Ministers for Defence of the Reich. Hitler decreed on the outbreak of war on 1 September 1939 that Hermann Goring was his official successor and named Hess as next in line. In addition to appearing on Hitler's behalf at speaking engagements and rallies, Hess signed into law much of the government's legislation, including the Nuremberg Laws of 1935, which stripped Jewish citizens of all rights in the lead-up to the Holocaust.

On 10 May 1941, Hess made a solo flight to Scotland, where he hoped to arrange peace talks with the Duke of Hamilton, whom he believed to be a prominent opponent of the British government's war policy. The British authorities arrested Hess immediately on his arrival and held him in custody until the end of the war when he was returned to Germany to stand trial at the 1946 Nuremberg trials of major war criminals. During much of his trial, Hess claimed to be suffering from amnesia, but he later admitted to the court that this had been a ruse. The court convicted him of crimes against peace and of conspiracy with other German leaders to commit crimes. He served a life sentence in Spandau Prison. When the Soviet Union blocked repeated attempts by family members and prominent politicians to procure his early release, while still in custody as the only prisoner in Spandau, he hanged himself in 1987 at the age of 93.

The Jesuit priest, a disciple of Lucifer was seeking to put into play his template of a Fourth Reich for our times. He was all too familiar with the fact that a One World Order was for many decades in play, with existing membership of Elite officials in governments, royalty and religious radicals. He was certain he could manipulate them and use his followers to instal a better outcome for world domination. This is why he was keen to investigate those under Hitler's leadership of the Third Reich, looking at where they went wrong, to ensure that his plan and subordinates didn't make similar mistakes. He turned to the next leader of Hitler's subordinates, Reinhard Heydrich, for he knew that an Armageddon of equal intensity was sure to follow once he put his plan into action. It would be another Holocaust of a different intensity and he would need an intelligence commander of Heydrich's standing to oversee the day-to-day running of the modern-day killing squadron in this Nuclear Age. So it was that he turned to review a brief on Heydrick with the knowledge that unlike his fellow leaders of the Reich he didn't commit suicide.

Reinhard was one of the key figures behind the Holocaust, He began his Nazi career in 1931 when Heinrich Himmler gave him the task to establish an intelligence wing of the SS, which resulted in the SD- Security Service which became responsible for rooting out political enemies of the Reich, and in 1934 Heydrich combined this rule in heading up the Gestapo which was founded by his Police Chief Himmler.

Beginning in April 1934, and at Hitler's request, Heydrich and Himmler began building a dossier on Sturmabteilung (SA) leader Ernest Rohm to remove him as a rival for party leadership and other political rivals At Hitler's direction, Heydrich, Himmler, Göring, and Viktor Lutz drew up lists of those who should be killed, starting with seven top SA officials and including many more. On 30 June 1934, the SS and Gestapo acted in coordinated mass arrests that continued for two days. Röhm was shot without trial, along with the leadership of the SA. The purge became known as the Night of the Long Knives. Up to 200 people were killed in the action. Lutze was appointed SA's new head and it was converted into a sports and training organisation.

With the SA out of the way, Heydrich began building the Gestapo into an instrument of fear. The Gestapo Law passed in 1936, gave police the right to act extra-legally. This led to the sweeping use of Schutzhalf-"protective custody", a euphemism for the power to imprison people without judicial proceedings. The courts were not allowed to investigate or interfere. The Gestapo was considered to be acting legally as long as it was carrying out the leadership's will. People were arrested arbitrarily, sent to concentration camps, or killed.

In early 1936, Heydrich left the Catholic Church in favour of a Higher Power movement under the influence of Heinrich Himmler's view. His wife, Lina, had already done so the year before. Heydrich not only felt he could no longer be a member but came to consider the church's political power and influence a danger to the state. All police forces throughout Germany were united, following Hitler's appointment of Himmler as Chief of the German Police. With this appointment sanctioned by Hitler, Himmler and his *de facto* deputy, Heydrich, became two of the most powerful men in the internal administration of Germany.[65] Himmler immediately reorganised the police into two groups: the Order Police; Orpo, consisting of both the national uniformed police and the municipal police, and the Security Police; SiPo), consisting of the *Geheime Staatspolizei* (Secret State Police; Gestapo) and (Criminal Police; Kripo. At that point, Heydrich was head of the SiPo and SD. Heinrich Muller was the Gestapo's operations chief.

Heydrich was assigned to help organise the 1936 Summer Olympics in Berlin. The games were used to promote the propaganda aims of the Nazi regime. Goodwill ambassadors were sent to countries that were considering a boycott. Anti-Jewish violence was forbidden for the duration, and newsstands were required to stop displaying copies of Der Sturmer. For his part in the games' success, Heydrich was awarded the *Deutsches Olympiaehrenzeichen* or German Olympic Games Decoration (First Class)

In January 1937, Heydrich directed the SD to secretly begin collecting and analysing public opinion and report back its findings He then had the Gestapo carry out house searches, arrests, and interrogations, thus in effect exercising control over public opinion. In February 1938 when the Austrian Chancellor Kurt Schushnigg resisted Hitler's proposed merger with Germany, Heydrich intensified the pressure on Austria by organising Nazi demonstrations and distributing propaganda in Vienna emphasising the common Germanic blood of the two countries. In the *'Joining'* on 12 March, Hitler declared the unification of Austria with Nazi Germany.

In mid-1939, Heydrich created the Stiflung Nordhav Foundation to obtain real estate for the SS and Security Police to use as guest houses and vacation spots. The Wannsee Villa, which the Stiftung Nordhav acquired in November 1940, was the site of the Wannsee Conference (20 January 1942). Heydrich was the lead speaker. At Wannsee, senior Nazi officials formalised plans to deport and exterminate all Jews in German-occupied territory and those countries not yet conquered. This action was to be coordinated among the representatives from the Nazi state agencies present at the meeting.

On 27 September 1939, the SD and SiPo—made up of the Gestapo and the Criminal Police, or Kripo—were folded into the new Reich Security Main Office or *Reichssicherheitshauptamt* (RSHA), which was placed under Heydrich's control. The title of *Chef der Sicherheitspolizei und des SD* (Chief of Security Police and SD) or CSSD was conferred on Heydrich on 1 October. Heydrich became the president of the International Criminal Police Commission (later known as Interpol) on 24 August 1940, and its headquarters were transferred to Berlin. He was promoted to SS-Obergruppenfuhrer *und General der Polizei* on 24 September 1941.

In 1936, Heydrich learned that a top-ranking Soviet officer was plotting to overthrow Joseph Stalin. Sensing an opportunity to strike a blow at both the Soviet Army and Admiral Canaris of Germany's Abwehr, Heydrich decided that the Soviet officer should be "unmasked". He discussed the matter with Himmler and both in turn brought it to Hitler's attention. Hitler approved Heydrich's plan to act immediately. But the "information" Heydrich had received was misinformation planted by Stalin himself in an attempt to legitimise his planned purges of the Red Army's high command. Stalin ordered one of his best NKVD agents, General Nikolai Skoblin, to pass Heydrich false information suggesting that Marshal Tukhachevsky and other Soviet generals were plotting against Stalin.

Heydrich's SD forged documents and letters implicating Tukhachevsky and other Red Army commanders. The material was delivered to the NKVD. The Great Purge of the Red Army followed Stalin's orders. While Heydrich believed they had deluded Stalin into executing or dismissing 35,000 of his officer corps, the importance of Heydrich's part is a matter of conjecture. Soviet military prosecutors did not use SD forged documents against the generals in their secret trial; they instead relied on false confessions extorted or beaten out of the defendants.

By late 1940, German armies had invaded most of Western Europe. The following year, Heydrich's SD was given responsibility for carrying out the Night-and-Fog decree. According to the decree, "persons endangering German security" were to be arrested in a maximally discreet way: "under the cover of night and fog". People disappeared without a trace with no one telling of their whereabouts or fate. For each prisoner, the SD had to fill in a questionnaire that listed personal information, country of origin, and the details of their crimes against the Reich. This questionnaire was placed in an envelope inscribed with a seal reading "Nacht und Nebel" and submitted to the Reich Security Main Office (RSHA). In the "Central Inmate File", as in many camp files, these prisoners would be given a special "covert prisoner" code, as opposed to the code for POW, Felon, Jew, Gypst, etc. The decree remained in effect after Heydrich's death. The exact number of people who vanished under it has never been positively established, but it is estimated to be 7,000.

CHAPTER 6.

THE RULERS OF TERROR

Heydrich created the "Zentralstelle IIP Polen" unit of the Gestapo to coordinate the ethnic cleansing of Poles in "Operation Tannenberg" and the Intelligenzaktion, two codenames for extermination actions directed at the Polish people during the German occupation of Poland. Among the 100,000 people murdered in the *Intelligenzaktion* operations in 1939–1940, approximately 61,000 were members of the Polish intelligentsia: scholars, clergy, former officers, and others, whom the Germans identified as political targets.

Heydrich came to Prague to enforce policy, fight resistance to the Nazi regime, and keep up production quotas of Czech motors and arms that were "extremely important to the German war effort." He viewed the area as a bulwark of Germany and condemned the Czech resistance's "stabs in the back". To realise his goals, Heydrich demanded racial classification of those who could and could not be German.. He explained, "Making this Czech garbage into Germans must give way to methods based on racist thought."

Reinhard Heydrich was a man of authority now and started his rule of turning the 'Czech garbage' as he called the people by terrorising the population. He proclaimed martial law and 142 people were executed within five days of his arrival in Prague. Their names appeared on posters throughout the occupied country Most of them were the members of the resistance that had previously been captured and were awaiting trial. According to Heydrich's estimate, between 4,000 and 5,000 people were arrested and between 400 and 500 were executed by February 1942. Those who were not executed were sent to Mauthausen- a concentration camp, where only four per cent of Czech prisoners survived the war. Czech Prime Minister Alois Elias was among those arrested the first day. He was put on trial in Berlin and sentenced to death but was kept alive as a hostage. He was later executed in retaliation for Heydrich's assassination.

In March 1942, further sweeps against Czech cultural and patriotic organisations, the military, and the intelligentsia resulted in the practical paralysis of the London-based Czech resistance. Almost all avenues through which Czechs could express the Czech culture in public were closed. Although small disorganised cells of Centra Leadership of Home resistance survived, only the communist resistance was able to function in a coordinated manner (although it also suffered arrests. The terror also served to paralyse resistance in society, with public and widespread reprisals by the Nazis against any action resisting German rule.[96]Heydrich's brutal policies during that time quickly earned him the nickname "the Butcher of Prague". The reprisals are referred to by Czechs as the *Heydrichiáda*.

As Acting Reich Protector of Bohemia and Moravia, Heydrich applied carrot and stick methods. Labour was reorganised based on the German Labour force. Heydrich used equipment confiscated from the Czech gymnastics organisation Sokol to organise events for workers. Food rations and free shoes were distributed, pensions were increased, and (for a time) free Saturdays were introduced. Unemployment insurance was established for the first time. The black market was suppressed. Those associated with it or the resistance movement were tortured or executed. Heydrich labelled them "economic criminals" and "enemies of the people", which helped gain him support. Conditions in Prague and the rest of the Czech lands were relatively peaceful under Heydrich, and industrial output increased. Still, those measures could not hide shortages and increasing inflation; reports of growing discontent multiplied.

Despite public displays of goodwill towards the populace, privately Heydrich was very clear about his eventual goal: "This entire area will one day be German, and the Czechs have nothing to expect here." Eventually up to two-thirds of the populace were to be either removed to regions of Russia or exterminated after Nazi Germany won the war. Bohemia and Moravia faced annexation directly into the German Reich.

The Czech workforce was exploited as Nazi-conscripted labour. More than 100,000 workers were removed from "unsuitable" jobs and conscripted by the Ministry of Labour. By December 1941, Czechs could be called to work anywhere within the Reich. Between April and November 1942, 79,000 Czech workers were taken in this manner for work within Nazi Germany. Also, in February 1942, the work day was increased from eight to twelve hours.

Heydrich was, for all intents and purposes, the military dictator of Bohemia and Moravia. His changes to the government's structure left President Emil Hachaand and his cabinet virtually powerless. He often drove alone in a car with an open roof – a show of his confidence in the occupation forces and his government's effectiveness. On 27 September 1941, Heydrich was appointed Deputy Reich Protector of the Protectorate of Bohemia and Morovia (the part of Czechoslovakia incorporated into the Reich on 15 March 1939) and assumed control of the territory. Upon his appointment, Heydrich told his aides: "We will Germanise the Czech vermin."This involved mass arrests of partisans, the use of Czech slave labour and the suppression of Czech cultural activities. Heydrick oversaw the mobile killing squads in Eastern Europe and was further charged with the task of devising a " final solution to the Jewish Question."

By 3 October 1941, Czechoslovak military intelligence in London had decided to kill Heydrich. On 20th January 1942, he chaired the famous Wannsee Conference which detailed the arrangements for the physical extermination of European Jewry. In May 1942, Heydrich's car was blown up by members of the Czech resistance and he died of injuries a week later. In death he was commemorated as a martyr to the cause, receiving a grand state funeral. The construction of the first purpose-built extermination camps at Belx zec, Sobibor and Treblinka became codenamed "Operation Reinhard" in his honour, while the two Chez villages under Hitler's orders were slaughtered in a brutal act of reprisal for his assassination.

So Father Olios then turned his attention to Reinhard's co-comrade in the terror and slaughters of millions, one Heinrich Himmler. He was gaining a clear understanding of the mindset of these cohorts of Adolf Hitler's Third Reich and their part in its demise. He began to read a brief of the man Heinrich Himmler, who joined the Nazi Party in 1925 and became one of Adolf Hitler's earliest followers, alongside Joseph Goebbels and Hermann Göring. As commander of the German *Schutzstaffel* (Protective Squadron), abbreviated SS, he created and controlled Nazi concentration camps and was responsible for the murder of more than 12 million people who were considered enemies by the Nazis.*

Himmler was born in Munich, Germany, to a pious, authoritarian Catholic schoolmaster in 1900. In 1918, after finishing school, he enlisted to fight in World War I, but the war ended before he saw combat. He then earned a degree in agriculture from the Technical University in Munich and found work as a fertiliser salesman. He joined the *Freikorps*, private armies of right-wing veterans who were resentful of Germany's loss in World War I. In 1923 Himmler joined the Nazi Party, which was recruiting *Freikorps* soldiers for the *Sturmabteilung* (Storm Troop), abbreviated SA, to protect senior leaders of the Nazi Party at public events. After the Beer Hall Putsch, the Nazi Party's failed push for power in Munich, the German government abolished the SA. Yet it was reestablished 15 months later along with the SS, which protected Nazi Party leaders throughout Germany. In January 1929 Himmler was appointed head of the SS, a small body of 200 men that he would soon transform into the racist and deadly army of the Nazi police state.

By 1933 Himmler's SS numbered 52,000 members of Hitler's "master race." Himmler then began a massive effort to separate the SS from the SA. To distinguish his troops, he introduced black SS uniforms that were unlike the SA's brown shirts. On June 30, 1934, under Hitler's orders, Himmler and Göring arranged the murder of SA leader Ernst Röhm and other senior SA officials in a massacre that would become known as The

Night of the Long Knives. As a result, Himmler became chief of the German Police, including the Gestapo, the secret police.

Coupling his power with a fanatical belief in the racist Nazi ideology, Himmler then organised and administered Nazi Germany's extermination camps. During a speech on October 4, 1943, Himmler remarked: "It is one of those things that is easily said. 'The Jewish people is being exterminated,' every Party member will tell you, clear, it's part of our plans, we're eliminating the Jews, exterminating them, a small matter.'" Himmler toured the Nazi camps often and personally witnessed many mass shootings, unlike Hitler, who never visited the camps.

By 1945 Himmler's Waffen-SS, a military branch formed in 1940, numbered 800,000 troops, but he had lost all hope for a German victory. Believing the Nazis needed to seek peace to survive, he contacted Count Folke Bernadotte of Sweden and began negotiations. Hitler declared Himmler a traitor and stripped him of all titles and ranks. After Hitler's death, Himmler contacted Supreme Allied Commander General Dwight Eisenhower and again offered to surrender if he could be spared prosecution as a Nazi leader. Instead, the Allies declared him a major war criminal. He was scheduled to stand trial at Nuremberg, but he committed suicide by swallowing a cyanide capsule before the interrogation. His last words were, "I am Heinrich Himmler!"

Father Schicklgurber, the Jesuit priest and leader of a cult of followers was coming to some eye-opening conclusions about the Nazi propaganda and the ultimate failure of the Third Reich regime. He was coming to believe that his great-grandfather, Adolf Hitler was not the all-powerful leader that he had claimed to be. He was a puffed-up creation for the masses of Germans to idolise but in truth, his image and the Reich itself was a false flag doomed to failure on more than one front. The history books told another story:

[Much of Nazi propaganda was devoted to portraying the regime as a streamlined state, with a pyramid of power culminating in the figure of the *Führer* at its peak, Hitler as the strong leader above the political fray. Presented as a positive image at the time, this picture of the regime was simply given a different, negative shading in post-war representations of the Third Reich as totalitarian, with one leader, one party and one ideology dominating the population through a monopoly of the means of propaganda and coercion. This image of Hitler as the almost archetypal *'strong dictator'* has perhaps pervaded popular images of Hitler ever since, as well as presenting a continuing thread in the historiography. Yet even contemporary observers recognised that the structures of power in the Third Reich were not quite this simple, and the duality of old state structures and new Party organisations led Ernst Fraenkel, for example, to speak of a *'dual state'*. Later historians, such as Edward Peterson, have focussed on what they perceive as the *'limits of Hitler's power'* and have characterised Hitler as being a *'weak'* dictator.] *

[The evidence for Hitler as a *'weak'* dictator rests in part on his style of political leadership and the changing institutional structure of politics. When not *'enacting power'*, as in the party rallies and public ceremonies, Hitler appeared to lack interest in the day-to-day details of policy and legislation. Cabinet government fell into disuse, and on many matters, Hitler tended simply to agree with the last person who had succeeded in *'catching his ear'*, or having a word with him when he was in a good mood. Patterns of political decision-making appear to have become increasingly haphazard, and competing centres of power proliferated, characterised by personal rivalries and animosities. Powerful underlings developed the empire. All this would suggest that Hitler's role was that of a *'weak'* dictator.] *

The post-war testimony of Hitler's former adjutant, Fritz Weidermann, lent credence to his lack of interest in the affairs of day-to-day government: " He [Hitler] disliked the study of documents. I have sometimes secured decisions from him, even ones about important matters, without his ever asking to see relevant files. He took the view that many things sort themselves out on their own if one did not interfere." In a similar vein, the head of the Reich Chancellery, Hans Lammers, admitted in a 1938 newspaper article that it was part of his duties to keep " peripheral matters" away from Hitler. Given these working practices, Structuralists have pondered whether Hitler left himself open to undue influence from those around him, thereby weakening his grip on the policy direction of the Third Reich.

Such a view contrasts strongly with the interpretation presented by those who emphasise Hitler's intentions and *'world view'* - *Weltanscaaung* - as being at the centre of the development of policies in the Third Reich. For *'Hitler-centric'* historians such as Hillgruber or Hildebrand, the goals of world conquest and racial extermination must and can only be explained primarily in terms of Hitler's intentions. Hitler remained a *'strong'* dictator.

The two views of Hitler's role were rooted in wider differences in the interpretation of the power structures of the Third Reich. On the one hand, for all the explicit attacks on the concept, the notion of a totalitarian state in which Hitler effectively exercised absolute power still lay, if only implicitly, behind much writing on the Third Reich. War and genocide could be explained primarily in terms of Hitler's intentions, carried out once the opportunity was ripe; the *'Hitler order' (Führer Befehl)* remained the focus of explanation. On the other hand, building on the work of Hans Mommsen and Martin Broszat, historians began to conceive of the Nazi state as *'polycratic'*: characterised by increasing competition between overlapping centres of power; a state in which politics became ever less a matter of formal procedures within clearly defined institutional structures and more a matter of personal rivalries among members of the elite.

Taken to an extreme in the so-called *'intentionalist/functionalist debate'* over the origins of the Holocaust, the internationalists seemed to incriminate only Hitler and a relatively small circle of loyal henchmen, while the structuralist emphasis on the *'cumulative radicalisation'* of the regime (which seemed to take on a momentum of its own) almost seemed to write Hitler out of the script altogether.

A close examination of Hitler's role in the Third Reich, as carried out by Ian Kershaw in his masterly two-volume biography of Hitler, develops a more complex model that succeeds in reconciling a focus on Hitler's supreme role with an analysis of the far from streamlined power structures of the dictatorship. Ian Kershaw points to ways in which Hitler's role as charismatic Führer was, almost paradoxically, itself in part a product of the increasingly chaotic structures of power; there was simply no other ultimate source of decision-making, and the *'Hitler order'* was the only final authority that could be cited. At the same time, the notion of *'working towards the Fuhrer'* (which Kershaw takes from a contemporary source) encapsulates how Hitler's undoubted personal power and extraordinary hold over his close followers stimulated actions *'from below'* that did not always require specific orders from above. It is possible in this way to synthesise the notion of power governed by many., riddled by internal rivalries, with that of Hitler's supreme role at the centre, shaping the parameters and ultimate goals of the regime.

Thus for example, while Hitler remained uninterested in the details of economic policy, he insisted on empowering Goering's *'Four year Plan'* office when the traditional economics of Hjalmar Schacht told him he could not prepare for war within four years while keeping domestic consumers happy. When there were squabbles among civil servants about how precisely to interpret the applicability of those to be affected by the Nuremberg Laws of *1935*, Hitler kept out of the debates until all sides were exhausted and willing to accept his ultimate verdict; at which point, true to his Darwinist principles, he supported the emergent (and in this case more moderate) winning side. The effect was to ratchet up anti-semitic policies one notch further towards exclusion from the *'Aryan' 'national community'* or *Volksgemeinschaft*, and ultimately, in the longer term, from Germany and from life itself. When the areas that were closest to Hitler's heart - expansionist foreign goals and aggressive racial policies - are examined, it is clear that Hitler never compromised in pursuit of his ultimate aims, however much he trimmed the details of the route according to circumstances and constraints. Yet at the same time, the circles of those implicated in the realisation of these policies must be spread far wider than the internationalist case would suggest. The structure of the regime mattered too.

Was Hitler then a *'weak'* dictator? In matters where the details did not concern him, arguably yes; but where the outcome mattered, rather than the minutiae of the route which was chosen, no. Is he then, conversely, to be characterised as a 'strong' dictator? Not if this means a reversion to the discredited notion of a streamlined *'totalitarian'* state, in which all power emanated from above and those below were simply forced to *'obey the Hitler orders'*. The realities are more complex than either side of this debate would at first suggest.

Soon after becoming chancellor Hitler used his power of the state to crack down on political opponents. He primarily targeted those on the left. To frighten middle-class Germans, Nazi propagandists spread rumours of an impending Communist plot to seize power. They even blamed an arsonist's burning of the German parliament building on the communists.

As a result, the government suspended basic civil rights for all German citizens, including rights such as freedom of expression, press, and assembly. Police and Nazi paramilitary units arrested Communists and social democrats. In 1933, they detained as many as 100,000 Germans without trial. Nazi thugs publicly humiliated, tortured, and killed people deemed to be enemies. The game was afoot for a new order of dictatorial government and police state control in Germany that would spread throughout Europe until the Nazi flame of control was extinguished in 1945.

When Hitler was appointed Chancellor of Germany in 1933 the Nazi party forced organisations, political parties, and state governments into line with Nazi goals. In the first months of his chancellorship, Hitler began a concerted policy of "synchronisation," and placing them under Nazi leadership. Culture, the economy, education, and law came under greater Nazi control. Trade unions were abolished and workers, employees, and employers were forced into Nazi organisations. By mid-July 1933, the Nazi Party was the only political party permitted in Germany. The Reichstag (German parliament) became a rubber stamp for Hitler's dictatorship. Hitler's will became the foundation for government policy.

The appointment of Nazi Party members to government positions increased Hitler's authority over state officials. According to the Nazi Party's leadership principle, authority flowed down from above and absolute obedience towards one's superior was expected at each level of the Nazi hierarchy. Hitler was the master of the Third Reich.

After claiming that the Communists committed arson that destroyed the Reichstag (German parliament) building in Berlin, Adolf Hitler used the incident to assume extraordinary powers in Germany. Hitler convinces the German president, Paul von Hindenburg, to declare a state of emergency. Constitutionally protected personal freedoms are thus suspended.

CHAPTER 7.

GERMANY UNDER THE 3rd REICH

Despite the state of emergency declared in February 1933 and the extraordinary powers assumed by Adolf Hitler, the Nazis fail to win a governing majority in parliamentary elections. The Nazis won only about 45 per cent of the vote. Later in March 1933, Hitler introduced a bill that would give his government the power to decree laws without submitting them to a vote in the German parliament. The bill passed in part because of the arrest of many Communist and Socialist opponents before the vote on the bill.

After the failure of the Nazi Party to win a majority in parliament, Adolf Hitler introduces a bill that would give his government legislative authority. The Nazis, the Conservatives, and the Catholic Center Party support this so-called "Enabling Act," which would grant Hitler's government the power to decree laws without a vote in parliament for four years. Communists and many Socialist opponents were arrested before the vote. In the end, only the remaining Socialists oppose the measure. The bill passes. Hitler soon outlaws all political parties in Germany—except the Nazi Party.

A purge of the Storm Trooper (SA) leadership and other supposed opponents of Adolf Hitler's regime takes place. This purge comes to be known as the "Night of the Long Knives." More than 80 SA leaders are arrested and shot without trial. Hitler claimed that the purge was a response to a plot by the SA to overthrow the government. The SA, under the leadership of Ernst Roehm, had sought to take the place of the German army. The removal of Roehm wins Hitler greater support from the army.

Upon the death of German President Paul von Hindenburg who died at the age of 87, Adolf Hitler took over the powers of the presidency. He had the army swear an oath of personal loyalty to him. Hitler's dictatorship thus rests on his position as Reich President-head of state, Reich Chancellor, head of government, and

Fuhrer, leader of the Nazi Party. Hitler's official title is now "Fuhrer and Reich Chancellor."

The first concentration camps in Germany were established soon after Adolf Hitler was appointed chancellor in January 1933. The Storm Troopers (SA) and the police established concentration camps beginning in February 1933. These camps were set up to handle the masses of people arrested as alleged political opponents. They were established on the local level throughout Germany. Gradually, most of these early camps were disbanded and replaced by centrally organised concentration camps under the exclusive jurisdiction of the SS (; the elite guard of the Nazi state). was the only concentration camp opened in 1933 that remained in operation until 1945, and was the model for the Nazi concentration camp system that replaced the earlier camps.

The Dachau camp, located near Munich in southern Germany, is one of the first concentration camps established by the Nazis. SS chief Heinrich Himmler announced its opening on March 20, 1933. The first prisoners arrive on March 22. They are mainly Communists and Socialists. Dachau is the only camp to remain in operation from 1933 until 1945.

Soon after the opening of the Dachau concentration camp in Munich, Adolf Hitler appointed SS chief Heinrich Himmler chief of all German police units with all police powers now centralised. The Gestapo (German secret state police) comes under Himmler's control. Responsible for state security, gave Himmler the authority to send individuals to concentration camps and members of His Gestapo were often also members of the SS.

The Nazi focus initially on the imprisonment of Communists and Socialists soon expanded to the imprisonment of and ultimately the extermination of Jews. Much of the early resources to feed the people of Germany came from the plunder of Jewish wealth. In general, rationing was accepted with little opposition, especially as food rations were reasonably generous until the middle of the war. Indeed, some people ate better during the war. However, in the last year of the war, ration cards were no longer honoured and shortages of food and clothing were server. During the Second World War, many Germans died because of the bombing by the Allies which destroyed their homes. Another problem faced by the German people as war raged on was that food became even more scarce and many resorted to eating animals and even dead war horses.

Germany had four key fatal weaknesses in the Second World War. These were: the lack of productivity on the home front to bolster the war economy, the weak supply lines, the start of a war on two fronts, and the lack of strong leadership were the causes of the Third Reich's ultimate failure. Following the invasion of the Soviet Union, using the Blitzkrieg tactic- a swift attack with a major force- the German Army marched far into Russia. However, they did so on very slow, overextended, supply lines. These supply lines hindered the German advance, and eventually led to a huge lack of supplies on the front line. This, alongside key Soviet advances, contributed to the German retreat.

In addition to the poor supply lines, Germany's war economy could not support the extent of goods needed for the various invasions in the Second World War. As Richard Evans writes, in Germany 'by 1944, 75 per cent of GDP was being devoted to the war in comparison to 60 per cent in the Soviet Union and 55 per cent in Britain' [Richard Evans, *The Third Reich at War*, (England: Penguin Group, 2008), p333]. Throughout the war, Germany became desperately short of fuel, coal and food. It was not until Albert Speer became Minister of Armaments and War Production in 1942 that Germany started moving towards a total mobilisation of the economy for war, although this was still with mixed success. In mid-1944 the economy peaked. For Nazi Germany, in retreat with a defensive war being fought on two fronts, this was too late. Following the Allies' D-Day offensive and the simultaneous Soviet offensive Operation Bagration, Germany was fighting a defensive war on the eastern front and the western front. This meant that the German troops were split, and neither side could have the full weight of the army. As a result of this, the German troops were pushed back into Germany.

In the post-war era, the military search service Deutsche Dienststelle (WaSt) was responsible for providing information to the families of those military personnel who were killed or went missing in the war. They maintained the files of over 18 million men who served in the war. By the end of 1954, they had identified approximately 4 million military dead and missing (2,730,000 dead and 1,240,629 missing). After German reunification, the records kept in the former German Democratic Republic of East Germany became available to the WASt. The German Red Cross reported in 2005 that the records of the WASt showed total Wehrmacht losses to have been 4.3 million men (3.1 million dead and 1.2 million missing) in World War II. Their figures include men conscripted from Austria and conscripted ethnic Germans from lands in Eastern Europe. The German historian Rüdiger Overmans used the files of the WASt to conduct his research on German military casualties. According to a report published by the Reuters News Agency, on July 29 1945 highly confidential archives found at Flensburg, in the house of General Reinecke showed German losses up to November 30, 1944, as 3.6 million.

The Holocaust was the genocide of European Jews during World War 11. Between 1941 and 1945, Nazi Germany and its collaborators systematically murdered some six million Jews across occupied Europe, around two-thirds of Europe's Jewish population. The murders were carried out primarily through mass shootings and poison gas in extermination camps. Separate Nazi persecutions killed a similar or larger number of non-Jewish civilians and POWs; the term *Holocaust* is sometimes used to refer to the persecution of these other groups.

The Nazi Party was founded in the wake of the war, and its ideology is often cited as the main factor explaining the Holocaust. From the beginning, the Nazis—not unlike other nation-states in Europe—dreamed of a world without Jews, whom they identified as "the embodiment of everything that was wrong with modernity. The Nazis defined the German nation as a racial community unbounded by Germany's physical borders and sought to purge it of racially foreign and socially deficient elements.

The Nazi Party and its leader, Adolf Hitler, were also obsessed with reversing Germany's territorial losses and acquiring additional 'living space' in Eastern Europe for colonisation. These ideas appealed to many Germans. The Nazis promised to protect European civilisation from the Soviet threat. Hitler believed that Jews controlled the Soviet Union, as well as the Western powers, and were plotting to destroy Germany. The insane mission of Hitler and the Third Reich resulted in a World War fatality statistics vary, with estimates of fatality deaths ranging from 50 million to more than 80 million. civilians. This represents the most military deaths of any nation by a large margin.] *

Father Schicklgurber sat at his office window overlooking St Peter's Square at Vatican City. He was deep in contemplating the realisation that all his plans for a Fourth Reich were being implemented without any input from him. The world was evolving towards an Armageddon of extreme intensity, far outweighing anything Hitler's Third Reich had envisaged. The New World Order was being implemented as constitutional rights, freedoms of citizens God-given rights, legal rights, natural rights of citizenship, unalienable rights and all civil liberties of human rights were being steadily taken away by an International Elite of rule makers with purpose-built stealth for what they perceived would be a better world for the selected few.

The priest had a clear picture now of a plan being implemented without any need for action by himself. Lucifer was winning hands down and the only comfort he had was that he was on his side. Fr Olios had no ego notations about his place in what was evolving, for it was akin to his plan of action in taking over the world. Such a plan of One World Order was of Grandfather Hitler's vision. \

Schicklguerber began to search through his papers for one of Hitler's prized racial ideological utterances and found the 1931 interview with a Leipzig newspaper editor. Adolf Hitler made a passionate declaration of the true significance of his National Socialist movement:

"The Frenchman Gobineau and the Englishman Chamberlain were inspired by our concept of a new order-a new order, I tell you, or if you prefer, an ideological glimpse into history by the basic principle of the blood. We do not judge by merely artistic or military standards or even by purely scientific ones. We judge by the spiritual energy that a people is capable of putting forth, which will enable it in ten years to recapture what it has lost in a thousand years of warfare. I intend to set up a thousand-year Reich and anyone who supports me in battle is a fellow fighter for a unique spiritual outcome would almost say divine creation. At the decisive moment, the decisive factor is not the ratio of strength but the spiritual force employed. Betrayal of the nation is possible even when no crime has been committed, in other words when a historical mission has not been fulfilled." *

It is evident to the priest from reading *Mein Kampf* and Hitler's speeches that he viewed racial conflict as the determining factor in all of human history. "The racial question gives the key not only to world history but to all human culture." Race was not simply a political issue to be used to curry the favour of the masses, but the "granite foundation" of Hitler's ideology.

CHAPTER 8.

THE MISSION OF WORLD DOMINION.

Hitler's racial ideology stemmed from what he called "the basic principle of the blood." This meant that the blood of every person and every race contained the soul of a person and likewise the soul of his race, the Volk. Hitler believed that the Aryan race, to which all "true" Germans belonged, was the race whose blood (soul) was of the highest degree. God Himself had created the Aryans as the most perfect men, both physically and spiritually. Since the blood (soul) of the Aryans contained specific spiritual energies, the "cultural energies" or "racial primal elements," as Hitler often called them, the Aryans supplied the culture that created the beauty and dignity of higher humanity. In other words, all that man calls higher culture was ultimately the product of the spiritual and creative energies that exist in the blood of the Aryans.

Hitler stated: "All the human culture, all the results of art, science, and technology that we see before us today, are almost exclusively the creative product of the Aryan. This very fact admits the unfounded inference that he alone was the founder of all higher humanity, therefore representing the prototype of all that we understand by the word "man." He is the Prometheus of mankind from whose bright forehead the divine spark of genius has sprung at all times... Exclude him perhaps after a few thousand years darkness will again descend on the earth, human culture will pass, and the world turn into a desert." He continued: "Human culture and civilisation on this continent are inseparably bound up with the presence of the Aryan. If he dies out or declines, the dark veils of an age without culture will again descend on this globe."

Fr Olios was at that moment feeling within his soul, and to some degree his DNA, the perceptions of his grandfather towards reality and God. Indeed, this dying-off of the Aryans was what Adolf Hitler perceived as happening around him. Germany's loss of World War I and subsequent economic problems were the visible contemporary evidence of Aryan decline. This descent occurred by the original sin of blood poisoning, or the contamination of the Aryan blood (soul) by an inferior race:" The Aryan gave up the purity of his blood and, therefore, lost his sojourn in the paradise which he had made for himself. He became submerged in the racial mixture, and gradually, more and more, lost his cultural capacity, until at last, not only mentally but also physically, he began to resemble the subjected aborigines more than his ancestors. Thus cultures and empires collapsed to make place for new formations. Blood mixture and the resultant drop in the racial level is the sole cause of the dying out of old cultures; for men do not perish as a result of lost wars, but by the loss of that force of resistance which is contained only in pure blood. All who are not of good race in this world are chaff."

The "serpent" that brought about the contamination of pure Aryan blood was, of course, the Jew. "The mightiest counterpart to the Aryan is represented by the Jew." To Hitler, the Jews were, of course, not members of a particular religious creed, but a specific race:

The Jew has always been a people with definite racial characteristics and never a religion; only to get ahead he early sought for a means that could distract unpleasant attention from his person. And what would have been more expedient and at the same time more innocent than the "embezzled" concept of a religious community? For here, too, everything is borrowed or rather stolen. Due to his original special nature, the Jew cannot possess a religious institution, if for no other reason because he lacks idealism in any form, and hence belief in a here-after is foreign to him. And a religion in the Aryan sense cannot be imagined which lacks the conviction of survival after death in some form.

From Hitler's perspective, the Jewish race was not created by God as one of the original root races of mankind and was, in his mind, un-Godly, inhuman, the embodiment of all that was evil. Hence the Jew " . . . stops at nothing, and in his vileness he becomes so gigantic that no one need be surprised if among our people the personification of the devil as the symbol for all evil assumes the living shape of the Jew." The goal of the

Jews was the domination of the world, a task that could be achieved by the poisoning of Aryan blood. Hitler contended that the Jews used a variety of methods to accomplish this task. The most blatant was miscegenation, accomplished by Jewish "rape" of Aryan girls and Jewish importation of Blacks into Germany to further destroy Aryan purity and carry out this kind of "disarming of the spiritually leading class "of his racial adversaries."

To Hitler, the Jewish race was also attempting to poison the Aryan blood (soul) by utilising social methods, such as cultural and political means. The Jew was the fundamental cause of the decadence that Hitler saw in modern art and literature. To Hitler, Jewish modem art was a deliberate attempt to infect the unconsciousness or inner self of the Aryan people. "Culturally he contaminates art, literature, the theatre, makes a mockery of natural feeling, overthrows all concepts of beauty and sublimity, of the noble and the good, and instead drags men down into the sphere of his base nature."

But it is in the area of politics that Hitler perceived the greatest Jewish threat to the Aryan race. Jewish infiltration of the bourgeoisie had made the latter puppets for the execution of the Jewish plan for world domination. Thus the bourgeois economic institution of capitalism and the political institutions of liberalism, democracy, parliamentarianism, freedom of the press, and internationalism were all Jewish instruments creating disorder in the world as a stepping stone to domination.

By far the most powerful political tool of the Jewish race, however, was Marxism. Marxism was a rival to individuals or groups that created a "view of life" directly hostile to everything in which Hitler believed. Marxism, to Hitler, maintained that the state had in itself the "creative, culture-forming force," meaning that the state created a nation's culture out of economic necessities.

In Hitler's view, the state could not create a nation's culture. Since the nation was the outward manifestation of a race's (Volk's) inner nature of the soul, the state then could only be the instrument by which a race could express its cultural energies. The state's primary function was to preserve and promote those Aryan culture-creating spiritual elements that existed in the blood of the Aryan race.

Hitler also deplored Marxism for its belief in racial equality. Racial inequality and Aryan domination did not permit such misunderstanding of the role of race in history. Likewise, Hitler denounced Marxism's levelling egalitarianism, which he felt destroyed the natural principle of inequality and the consequent domination of some individuals (an elite) over others. Hitler saw the Marxist threat to Aryan culture-creating ability not as coincidental but as a deliberate plan to destroy culture, bring civilisation into chaos, and enable the Jews to achieve their goal of world domination. To Hitler, "the Jew Karl Marx" knew precisely what policies would lead to world chaos.

Karl Marx was only the one among millions who, with the sure eye of the prophet, recognised in the morass of a slowly decomposing world the most essential poisons, extracted them, and, like a wizard, prepared them into a concentrated solution for the swifter annihilation of the independent existence of free nations on this earth. And all this in service of his race.

Hitler believed that his Nazi party, founded as a spiritual movement, would successfully rise to German political dominance since it was based in his mind on eternally true ideals rooted in the very soul of the Aryan race. Once in power, the Nazi movement could then create a state that would foster the historic destiny of the Aryan race. And the first task of this Aryan state would be to eliminate the Jewish threat.

This is why Hitler's political career both began and ended with a warning against the Jewish danger. In a letter dated 16 September 1919, called "the first piece of writing of Hitler's political career," Hitler was quite clear about his motives: the "ultimate goal [of a rational antifascism] must unalterably be the elimination of the Jews altogether." At the very end of his career, when he wrote his political testament to the German people, his preoccupation with the Jewish threat was still uppermost in his mind: "Above all, I bind the leadership of the nation and those under them to a meticulous observance of the racial laws and merciless opposition to the universal poisoners of all peoples, international Jewry."

The final solution of the "Jewish question," namely, the genocide of the Jewish race in Europe, takes on its proper significance as the final, logical product of Hitler's racial ideology. Once the Jew was purged from Europe, Germany would be able to produce pure Aryans who would be physically and spiritually perfect human beings. Thus Hitler's new order would be established with spiritually pure Aryans, demigod rulers, who, as Hitler enigmatically expressed it, "having achieved possession of this earth, will have a free path for activity in domains which will lie partly above it and partly outside it." This last statement is a reminder that Hitler suggested on occasion that there was a deeper, cosmic significance to his new order. "National Socialism," he once exclaimed to Otto Strasser, "would be worth nothing if it were restricted merely to Germany and did not seal the supremacy of the superior Race over the entire world for at least a thousand to two thousand years."

Father Olois then turned to Hitler's fascination with spiritual power and the occultism of his time, with which the priest was well familiar in his pursuits and worldview. He had turned to the paper writings of a woman who had studied this subject matter. [The original spirituality of man can be seen, according to Blavatsky, in the fact that mankind once was endowed with psychic powers, which she attributed to the so-called "Cyclopean eye." With the "Cyclopean eye" man had "spiritual sight," the ability to perceive subtle realities of the spiritual world, and thus could "see" into the future and read minds. Blavatsky felt that as man evolved materially and intellectually this "Third Eye" atrophied to what is now the pineal gland and man mostly lost his psychic powers. But, stated Blavatsky, mankind is destined to regain these abilities]*

That Hitler was well versed in these racial peculiarities is demonstrated in one of Herman Rauschning's conversations with Hitler: The pursuit of the "random path of the intelligence," we learned, was the real defection of man from his divine mission. To have "magic insight" was Hitler's idea of the goal of human progress. He felt that he already had the rudiments of this gift. He attributed to it his success and his future eminence. A savant of Munich ... had also written some curious stuff about the prehistoric world ... about forms of perception and supernatural powers. There was the eye of Cyclops or median eye, the organ of magic perception of the Infinite, now reduced to a rudimentary pineal gland. Speculations of this sort fascinated Hitler, and he would sometimes be entirely wrapped up in them. He saw his remarkable career as a confirmation of hidden powers. He saw himself as chosen for superhuman tasks, as the prophet of the rebirth of man in a new form.

According to Hitler, "Creation is not yet at an end, Man has arrived at a turning point... A new variety of man is beginning to separate." Hitler further believed that mankind would evolve into two distinct types. "The two types will rapidly diverge from one another. One will sink to a subhuman race and the other will rise far above the man of today. I might call the two varieties the god-man and the mass-animal." The new, godlike Aryan would rule over the inferior races, the "mass-animal."

To Hitler, it was the divine mission of the Nazi movement to bring this about: "Those who see in National Socialism nothing more than a political movement know scarcely anything of it. It is more even than a religion: it is the will to create mankind anew." To accomplish this Hitler believed that the Nazi movement must return the Aryan to his original state, for example, oneness with Volk, "herd instinct," racial purity, and inner spirituality. If the Nazi movement was to lead the Aryan race back to its purest form, it must, Hitler felt, eliminate those factors that caused it to stray in the first place. These are the intellect, egoism, materialism, and impurity of blood. The existence of these elements was not, in Hitler's mind, an accident of Aryan evolution, but the result of the conspiratorial actions of the Jews.

The scholarly Father Olois Shicklgurber noted in further reading of the work of Russian author Helena Blavatsky that she had helped to foster antisemitism, which is perhaps one of the reasons her esoteric work was so rapidly accepted in German circles. She sharply differentiated between Aryan and Jewish religion. The Aryans were the most spiritual people on earth. For them, religion was an "everlasting lodestar." For the Jews, religion was grounded on "mere calculation." They had a "religion of hate and malice toward everyone and everything outside itself." Jewish materialism and selfishness contrasted strongly with Aryan spirituality and selflessness. This dualism is dramatically echoed in Hitler in the following passage:

Two worlds face one another, men of God and the men of Satan. The Jew is the anti-man, the creature of another god. He must have come from another root of the human race. I set the Aryan and the Jew over against each other, and if I call one of them a human being I must call the other something else. The two are as widely separated as man and beast. Not that I would call the Jew a beast. He is much further from the beasts than we Aryans. He is a creature outside nature and alien to nature. Hitler's dualism, unlike Blavatsky's, was conceived simply as a conflict between two races: "The struggle for world domination will be fought entirely between us, between Germans and Jews."

The priest was considering the viewpoint of Hitler's warped belief in the extermination of the Jews. He remembered reading a report written by Major-General, Count Cherep-Spiridovich, a soldier, political activist and writer. He remembered he was a Russian count who had moved to the United States following the Bolshevik Revolution. He said he was a Tsarist General and Russian royalist and had been involved in Pan-Slavism, white Russian anti-semitic activism and had belonged to various civil orders and cultural organisations in both Russia and the USA. Among his papers in his extensive liberty, he found an early 20th-century newspaper clipping that stated "…there is a story and it is still unfolding, that there is a Satanist lust of murder that the world has embraced ever since the time of Christ. It was Jesus, our Saviour if one believes in the sacrifice he made on the Cross some two thousand years ago, who warned: "Gentiles keep away from Jews." and history daily confirms this. That is not to say that the average Jew in the everyday world should be shunned. Quite the opposite, they are the backbone of progress and good orderly direction that keeps things ticking over, and the majority that I've known over my lifetime are good people. No, it is not the everyday Jew that one must shun, it is those of a dark breed that shall be called here "The hand in the dark," for they are the personification of all that is evil and their goal is blood, death and destruction, thou they come dressed in sheep clothing seeking to fulfil the whim of their desires. "A One World Government that is, is a Hand in the Dark."

The Count had continued: "A statesman must know how to foresee the future. A politician grasps only the present, which is already the past. Those of that hidden hand have been the instrument of turning a nation against nation, against the will of God, and we the people have suffered the consequences of earthquakes of nature, commerce and disease, deceit, murder, lust and power consciousness, as a result of their ultimate evil intent. To govern is to foresee and whilst these Jews of the Hand in the Dark continue to wreak havoc on the world, through their lust for power and control, the masses of men lead lives of quiet desperation. " and then the punchline. "We must note the warning: The Talmud is today preached in every synagogue! it teaches: "Thou (Jew) shall smite the other nations, which the Lord delivers in your (Jewish) hands...kill the best of them."

The priest soon realised Hitler got it all wrong in the quest to rid the world of Jews, but in the essence of Christian theology and Jewish Masonic heritage, hatred and death on the surface seemed not to solve the racial question irrespective of which way one may view it. He was beginning to realise that his former religious theological thinking had some merit before he accepted the ways of Lucifer and the darkness of his soul's human character. For it was Lucifer's mission that darkness would win over light and death under his guidance was the quest. The Christian Mass, and indeed the Black Mass of his occult used symbolism and signs, just as effectively as Hitler and his cronies had marketed the Swastika, the Eagle and the Nazi Flag. But in the world of this current century turning back the clock to change was too late. The world of the rising sun of a Fourth Reich was already progressing at the speed of light towards a future Armageddon.

Father Olios read that 'The Count' went on to claim he had warned King Alexander 1 and the Queen of Serbia of their pending assassination before that 1902 event. He claimed he had warned Grand Duke Sergei Alexandrovich of Russia in 1904 of his pending assassination which happened in 1905. He also claimed he had foreseen WW 1 and WW 11 and future wars. The priest read of his links with the Slavonic Society of Russia and the Latino-Slavic League of Paris and Rome. His support of Tsar Nicholas 11 of Russia and his opposition to Bolshevism. Lord Alfred Douglas had written in an American newspaper that 'The Count' was well known to men like Henry Ford and other notables of the time. He had written a lot of pre-WW1 books and in seven of these, he became known as a political poetic prophet.

The British Financial Times had taken his predictions seriously and published him, where he reached a fairly wide international readership. Count Spiridovich had moved to Harlem, New York in 1920, where he was detained for special inquiry by the Immigration Bureau before being granted the right to live in the USA. In America, he opened a branch of the Anglo-Latino-Slav-league, where he advocated the unification of "white people of the globe against the domination of coloured peoples." He had also organised the Universal Gentiles League among Russians in the USA and wrote numerous Anti-Semitic leaflets on "The Secret World Government." He claimed he had the support of Henry Ford for his anti-semitic beliefs and had attempted to publish a book on the subject but was stopped by armed men posing as US Government officials.

The radical Catholic priest was reading a document of the account of the Russian Count who had died in suspicious circumstances in a Staten Island hotel, in October 1926. Those who had arranged to end his life knew his predictions of the economic outcome of the depression years and those of World War 11 that would take place. He was found in the hotel room with a gas pipe in his mouth attached to a gas tap in the room. The assumption that he had died by gassing himself to death would have been a reasonable assumption except for the fact that the gas in the hotel had been disconnected two years prior.

A stack of documents on the prophetic claims of the Russian-born Count Spiridocvich was piled up on the little Jesuit radical priest's desk. He was taking on board an insight into the prophet of the age, and began to read more: " ... some people of my time and even in the history books thought that I was anti-Semitic; they have misread my mission and belief. I have never worked nor wrote against the daily order of the Jewish people, but have always been against the protocol of the Elders of Zion. Some consider my views racist and that I was against the coloured man. They were mistaken, it was not the colour of the skin that I was referring to in my messages to the proletariat and Governments, but the darkness of the minds of the hidden hand that orchestrates and manipulates humanity to do foul deeds. Deeds that have and still do result in ultimate destruction, disease, and the murder of millions of suffering souls throughout the world. This was not, and still is not the Christian values that you and I and millions of others seek to live by. It is not the values that the masses of the Jewish people wish to live by either. It is the values system, however, of those that manipulate the world into evil and the works of Satan."

"It is the work of the Judeo-Mongols, who are composing the World Government, they are the hand in the dark of the Hidden Hand, the many who have made billions out of wars, in their lust of murder and deceit of the masses of humanity." They will continue to manipulate the world press and all forms of media, control the money flow, interfere with the climate blame the masses dumb down the education of our children, alter and adept the history books to their liking."

Father Olios had to admit that The Count in his prophetic messages was well tuned to the world scene of his era and had his finger on the pulse of the new age of today that is emerging. It seemed to him that the world was repeating what those Elite few of Jewish blood, and those who worked in the league within them, were still working towards that 20th-century mission of a One World Government to control all.

The not-so-innocent priest and theologian were busy doing some comparisons of the world of his grandfather Adolf Hitler and the emerging world of One World Order that was happening even as he read more of the Count's words: "Comparisons of the 3rd Reich and the emerging 4th Reich in its accent." Father Clios was acutely aware of the inevitable change and pending Armageddon that was to affect the world in the not-too-distant future. He knew he had but a small part to play in its happening as those of the dark side of world leadership have sold their soul to Satan in exchange for power, fame, pleasure and materialism. The priest was deeply depressed as to his lot in life now.

Although highly successful as a teacher and theologian, he was like the fictitious story of Faust, dissatisfied with his life. In evaluating how he fell from such a holy life to wallow in the baseness of his defects of character by making a pact with Lucifer. He was now at a crossroads having sold his soul for unlimited knowledge and the temporal life of the world. It dawned on the priest that it was in his DNA to pursue some of the traits of his grandfather Hitler, but he need not be like him at all. He knew that whilst he had made a bargain with the devil's magic powers, at the end of the term the Devil would claim his soul as he had done in the story of Faust. He had no intention of being eternally enslaved and for a brief moment contemplated suicide. But sanity prevailed as he began to reevaluate how far he had fallen and what he could do to redeem himself.

He was asking himself how he could let go, hand back all of his shortcomings to the God of his understanding and escape the grasp of his defective nature. As he had so often prayed to the congregation at Mass in his younger highly spiritual days: "Let us call to mind our sins." What part had he played in this link that he had with the occult evil goal of world domination? Had he not partaken in ritual sacrifice, offering a lamb to Satan? And had he not encouraged occult followers to drink the blood of the lamb and share the eating of the heart in a Black Mass with Lucifer?

CHAPTER 9.

THE REDEMPTION OF A RADICAL PRIEST

Olois Shicklgurber, Jesuit priest, made his way to the private room of the Pope and there he knelt before the Vicar of Christ on earth and poured out his sin. The Pope gave him absolution on the understanding that he would turn from the occult, close down the practice of Black Mass celebrations and seal the room as a tomb never to be reopened. For his penance, he was given the task to rid the Church of priests who abuse children. He had not himself been guilty of sexual misconduct with children, but he was mindful of those who did and it was now his task to change all this for the protection of children and to appease the souls of other religious who had turned to this evil practice.

Father Shicklgurber in his new state of grace returned to his room and searched for a book from his large collection of historic works. He opened a copy of The Maronite Poet, Gibran's book 'The Prophet', reflected in a poem the mystery of the child: "Your children are not yours. They are the sons and daughters of Life's longing for itself. They come through you but not from you. And though they are with you yet they belong not to you." He was thinking back on a press briefing during Pope Francis's visit to the USA in September 2015 when he met with survivors of sexual abuse. He stated quote: "God weeps for the sexual abuse of children." He celebrated the thought of sexual abuse of children as a universal problem in a Universal Church. He pondered over the thought that perhaps the closest historical parallel in church history of confessional soliciting was where, before and after the confessional box the priest confessor made sexual overtures or engaged in carnal activity with the penitent. This is how it was up to the time of the Spanish Inquisition.

Turning to a document on the Inquisition he noted a prominent journalist had written: "Instead of the more public ecclesiastical courts, the Spanish Inquisition trials were conducted in secrecy so that the nightmare of respected members of the clergy being brought to trial for solicitation and publicly excoriated could be avoided. Thus, by using the Inquisition, its proceedings were secret and even sentencing and reconciliation of offenders could be carried on behind closed doors. Throughout the centuries, the Church authorities strove massively to keep sexual topics away from public view. However, with the advent of radio and T.V. combined with the arrival of investigative journalism, the maintenance of such secrecy was always doomed to failure. Notwithstanding that the Crimean Solicitations ordered that canonical trials of clergy accused of solicitation, homosexuality, bestiality and child sexual abuse were to be covered by the 'permanent secret proceedings of the Holy Office', the penalty for violating was excommunication.'

The priest with his renewal of "Our Father's Holy Faith," had a new mission now to stamp out child abuse and rid the Church of those priests that tainted their priestly duty overcome with uncontrollable sexual desire. He knew that this was now to be his life purpose. The Pope could only do so much and he chose to turn his attention to educating young men and women to get behind his cause. He also felt he had a duty to those who were blind to the growing rise of the 4th Reich which had at its core Elites who involved themselves in all sorts of occult practices in the name of a new world order, of a One World Government, a Reich that would lead to an ultimate Armageddon before this decade had passed.

Father Schicklgruber put down his books and documents and retreated to his lounge room with a drink in hand, turning on the evening news. He was watching as President Biden signed legislation that incorporated the Rebuilding Economic Prosperity and Opportunity Act which empowers the President to seize Russian foreign exchange reserves within the U.S. after identifying reserves and reporting back to Congress within 180 days. He recalled as of mid-February 2024, the U.S. and its allies have sent $280 billion to Ukraine in military, financial, and humanitarian aid. Seizing Russian reserves helps allied governments continue to support Ukraine by reducing the burden on taxpayers and making Russia foot the bill for its aggression. Ukrainian President Volodymyr Zelensky has repeatedly urged allies to seize

Russian reserves, saying in January 2024, "The more billions [Putin] and his oligarchs, friends, and accomplices lose, the more likely he will regret starting this war." Finally, Russian reserves are appealing in their quantity; they would cover three-quarters of the cost of rebuilding Ukraine as estimated by the World Bank one year into the war. As former World Bank president Robert Zoellick writes, seizing reserves is "elegant justice" and a desperately needed infusion for Ukraine.

It was shades of what the Bank of International Settlements had done when the Bank of England records detailing its involvement in the transfer and sale of gold stolen by Nazis after the invasion of Czechoslovakia were revealed. The gold had been deposited during the 1930s with the Bank of International Settlements (BIS), the so-called Central Banker's bank, as the Czechoslovak government faced a growing threat from Germany. The document had gone on to detail how a request was made in March 1939 to transfer gold, then worth £5.6m, from a Czech National Bank account at the BIS to an account operated by Germany's Reichsbank. Some £4m in gold went to banks in the Netherlands and Belgium, while the rest was sold in London. The Czech gold was transferred to the Reich two months after The Nazi invasion of Czechoslovakia and now the same things were happening again. Putin had objected that it was illegal under International law but this didn't stop the powers that be to reenact what had been done before.

The priest was thinking now of identifying the parallels of what had happened with the 3rd Reich, how it had failed and how so many suffered. He could not in his good conscience allow this to happen again without reminding the hearts and minds of the people what was now transpiring. The world seems to be blind to the rise of a 4th Reich and to the all familiar patterns of Nazi Germany apparent in America. His ambitions for an occult to conquer all had been replaced by a new zeal to inform humankind of the steps that were now in progress to bring disorder and chaos on a rising trend towards world dictatorships as had happened in the past. He was reminded of the rise of the dictatorship of Joseph Stalin in Russia, Mussolini in Italy and Adolf Hitler in Germany, and of millions of lives lost. There seem to be too many parallels with Trump, Putin and Kim Jung Un to ignore. Mankind he decided needed a reminder of the terrible consequences of what happens when good men do nothing to change the course of history for the betterment of all. He would begin by informing his congregation at Mass, to awaken their spirits to mankind's God-given rights of people power. However, some doubts the priest had to himself: " Had mankind not progressed beyond a return to the dark days of WW1 and WW11?"

Reportedly the old secret society of the Jewish elite that founded and continued to fund political leaders, who wanted equally to bring down national governments of the free world in favour of Fascist totalitarian dictatorships was on the rise again. And they had no better pawn in the game than Donald Trump.

An article from a recent interview by a Times magazine journalist early in 2024 on a function organised by Trump aids to promote his return to power endorsed the anticipated leader of the American nation as heir apparent. Donald Trump was standing on the patio at Mar-a-Lago near dusk watching the well-heeled crowd eating Wagyu steaks and grilled fish pauses to applaud as he took his seat. On this gorgeous evening, the brotherhood was packed with an idealistic mecca of rich and famous elite donors to dining with the former President after a joint press conference proposing legislation to prevent non-citizens from voting. in federal elections is already illegal, and extremely rare, but remains a Trump fixation that the embattled guest speaker appeared happy to co-sign in exchange for the political cover that standing with Trump provides.

Trump's radical designs for presidential power would be felt throughout the country. The main focus is the southern border. Trump says he plans to sign orders to reinstall many of the same policies from his first term, such as the Remain in Mexico program, which requires that non-Mexican asylum seekers be sent south of the border until their court dates, and Title 42, which allows border officials to expel migrants without letting them apply for asylum. The pandemic-era ban, which began under former President Donald Trump in 2020 and has continued under Biden, has been a prominent approach to swiftly expel migrants.

The Biden administration in 2022 tried to phase out Title 42 but was blocked by a lawsuit filed by Republicans in 19 states. By the time it ended due to the expiration of the COVID-19 public health emergency, Biden was replacing Title 42 with an arguably tougher, more restrictive policy. His administration on Friday started implementing a rule barring migrants from asylum if they don't request refugee status in another country before entering the US. "This new rule is no less illegal or harmful. It will effectively eliminate asylum for nearly all non-Mexican asylum seekers who enter between designated ports of entry, and even for those who present at a port without first securing an appointment,"

A second-term Trump adviser says he plans to cite record border crossings and child-trafficking as justification for reimposing the emergency measures. He would direct federal funding to resume construction of the border wall, likely by allocating money from the military budget without congressional approval. The capstone of this program, advisers say, would be a massive deportation operation that would target millions of people. Trump made similar pledges in his first term but says he plans to be more aggressive in a second. "People need to be deported," says Tom Homan, a top Trump adviser and former acting head of Immigration and Customs Enforcement. "No one should be off the table."

Presidents typically have a narrow window to pass major legislation. Trump's team is eyeing two bills to kick off a second term: a border-security and immigration package, and an extension of his 2017 tax cuts. Many of the latter's provisions expire early in 2025: the tax cuts on individual income brackets, 100% business expensing, and the doubling of the estate-tax deduction. Trump is planning to intensify his protectionist agenda, telling me he's considering a tariff of more than 10% on all imports, and perhaps even a 100% tariff on some Chinese goods. Trump says the tariffs will liberate the U.S. economy from being at the mercy of foreign manufacturing and spur an industrial renaissance in the

U.S. When I point out that independent analysts estimate Trump's first term tariffs on thousands of products, including steel and aluminium, solar panels, and washing machines, may have cost the U.S. $316 billion and more than 300,000 jobs, by one account, he dismisses these experts out of hand. His advisers argue that the average yearly inflation rate in his first term—under 2%—is evidence that his tariffs won't raise prices.

'

CHAPTER 10.

THE SECOND COMING OF DONALD TRUMP

In the Times Mar-a-Lago interview, says he might fire U.S. Attorney Trump who refused his orders to prosecute someone: "It would depend on the situation." He's told supporters he would seek retribution against his enemies in a second term. This would include Fani Willis the Atlanta-area district attorney who charged him with election interference, and Alvin Bragg, the Manhattan DA in the Stormy Daniels case, who Trump has previously said should be prosecuted. Trump demurs but offers no promises. "No, I don't want to do that," he says, before adding, "We're gonna look at a lot of things. What they've done is a terrible thing."

Trump has also vowed to appoint a "real special prosecutor" to go after Biden. "I wouldn't want to hurt Biden," he tells me. "I have too much respect for the office." Seconds later, though, he suggests Biden's fate may be tied to an upcoming Supreme Court ruling on whether Presidents can face criminal prosecution for acts committed in office. "If they said that a President doesn't get immunity," says Trump, "then Biden, I am sure, will be prosecuted for all of his crimes." (Biden has not been charged with any, and a House Republican effort to impeach him has failed to unearth evidence of any crimes or misdemeanours, high or low.)

The spectacle picks up where his first term left off. The events of January 6, during which a pro-Trump mob attacked the centre of American democracy to subvert the peaceful transfer of power, were a profound stain on his legacy. Trump has sought to recast an insurrectionist riot as an act of patriotism. "I call them the J-6 patriots," he says. When I ask whether he would consider pardoning every one of them, he says, "Yes." As Trump faces dozens of felony charges, including for election interference, conspiracy to defraud the United States, wilful retention of national-security secrets, and falsifying business records to conceal hush-money payments, he has tried to turn legal peril into a badge of honour. Today he seems to be winning.

Ironically on July 1, 2024, the Supreme Court gave Donald Trump a partial win in his effort to establish presidential immunity, endorsing the expansive legal view that a president cannot be subject to criminal prosecution for anything they do in an "official capacity." The court's ruling means that Trump's January 6 case goes back to Federal Judge Tanya Chutkan, who had presided over it in her Washington courtroom before Trump's team appealed. Chutkan will now establish what part of Trump's efforts to overturn the 2020 election was "official" — but may be constrained by six justices' narrow interpretation of that word. And a trial date ahead of the presidential election is now all but impossible.

To supporters, the prospect of Trump's second term in office, unconstrained and backed by a disciplined movement of true believers, offers revolutionary promise. Too much of the rest of the nation and the world represents an alarming risk. A second Trump term could bring "the end of our democracy," says presidential historian Douglas Brinkley, "and the birth of a new kind of authoritarian presidential order."

Nowhere would that power be more momentous than at the Department of Justice. Since the nation's earliest days, Presidents have generally kept a respectful distance from Senate-confirmed law-enforcement officials to avoid exploiting for personal ends their enormous ability to curtail Americans' freedoms. But Trump, burned in his first term by multiple investigations directed by his appointees, is ever more vocal about imposing his will directly on the department and its far-flung investigators and prosecutors.

In a second term, Trump's influence on American democracy would extend far beyond pardoning powers. Allies are laying the groundwork to restructure the presidency in line with a doctrine called the unitary executive theory, which holds that many of the constraints imposed on the White House by legislators and the courts should be swept away in favour of a more powerful Commander in Chief.

Donald Trump thinks he's identified a crucial mistake of his first term: He was too nice. He had been talking for an hour on April 12 at his fever dream palace in Palm Beach. Aides lurk around the perimeter of a gilded dining room overlooking the manicured lawn. When one nudges the journalist to wrap up the interview, he brings up the many former Cabinet officials who refuse to endorse Trump this time. Some have publicly warned that he poses a danger to the Republic. Why should voters trust you, I ask, when some of the people who observed you most closely do not? As always, Trump punches back, denigrating his former top advisers. But beneath the typical torrent of invective, there is a larger lesson he has taken away. "I let them quit because I have a heart. I don't want to embarrass anybody," Trump says. "I don't think I'll do that again. From now on, I'll fire."

Six months from the 2024 presidential election, Trump is better positioned to win the White House than at any point in either of his previous campaigns. He leads Joe Biden by slim margins in most polls, including in several of the seven swing states likely to determine the outcome. But the interviewed had not come to ask about the election, the disgrace that followed the last one, or how he has become the first former—and perhaps future—American President to face criminal trials. He wanted to know what Trump would do if he won a second term, to hear his vision for the nation, in his own words.

What emerged in interviews by the Times journalist Eric Cortellesssa in April 2024 and conversations with more than a dozen of his closest advisers and confidants, were the outlines of an imperial presidency that would reshape America and its role in the world. To carry out a deportation operation designed to remove more than 11 million people from the country, Trump told him, he would be willing to build migrant detention camps and deploy the U.S. military, both at the border and inland. He would let red states monitor women's pregnancies and prosecute those who violate abortion bans. He would, at his discretion, withhold funds appropriated by Congress, according to top advisers. He would be willing to fire a U.S. Attorney who doesn't carry out his order to prosecute someone, breaking with a tradition of independent law enforcement that dates from America's founding. He is weighing pardons for every one of his supporters accused of attacking the U.S. Capitol on Jan. 6, 2021, more than 800 of whom have pleaded guilty or been convicted by a jury. He might not come to the aid of an attacked ally in Europe or Asia if he felt that country wasn't paying enough for its defence. He would gut the U.S. civil service, deploy the National Guard to American cities as he sees fit, close the White House pandemic-preparedness office, and staff his Administration with acolytes who back his false assertion that the 2020 election was stolen.

Trump remains the same guy, with the same goals and grievances. But in person, if anything, he appears more assertive and confident. "When I first got to Washington, I knew very few people," he says. "I had to rely on people." Now he is in charge. The arranged marriage with the timorous Republican Party stalwarts is over; the old guard is vanquished, and the people who remain are his people. Trump would enter a second term backed by a slew of policy shops staffed by loyalists who have drawn up detailed plans in service of his agenda, which would concentrate the powers of the state in the hands of a man whose appetite for power appears all but insatiable. "I don't think it's a big mystery what his agenda would be," says his close adviser Conway. "But I think people will be surprised at the alacrity with which he will take action."

Donald Trump has long toyed with the language of famous autocrats, authoritarians and fascists. Think: " enemy of the people," or "Retribution" and the more frequent years-long allusions to political violence. But even by his standards, the former president is now mining darker territory—with overtones of some of the ugliest episodes in recent world history. Trump not only likened his political opponents to "vermin" but suggested they represent a "threat from within" that is more dangerous than threats from beyond our borders. Both are themes seized upon by strongmen to foment populist movements.

Trump's campaign responded by seemingly taking issue with the "ridiculous" framing. But in the same breath, it also promised that Trump's "snowflake" critics' "entire existence will be crushed when President Trump returns to the White House." (It later sought to amend that to "sad, miserable existence.") As that response indicates, the campaign is not exactly apologising for this type of rhetoric, which is, at the very least and to be quite charitable, a calculated attempt at provocation. And after years of this kind of rhetoric and events like Jan 6, you could certainly forgive people for worrying that it's more than that.

"The language is the language that dictators use to instil fear," Timothy Naftali, a senior research scholar at Columbia University's School of International and Public Affairs, told The Washington Post. "When you dehumanise an opponent, you strip them of their constitutional rights to participate securely in a democracy because you're saying they're not human. That's what dictators do."

Just how similar is Trump's language to the actual words of those figures? Let's examine how his recent comments compare with Adolf Hitler's mission. Trump said Saturday: "We pledge to you that we will root out the communists, Marxists, fascists and the radical left thugs that live like vermin within the confines of our country, that lie and steal and cheat on elections." As The Post's story noted, likening one's political opponents and certain elements within the country to vermin and beasts was a tactic employed by Hitler.

Hitler used the construct to justify the extermination of Jews and to attack Marxists, while Trump has used it more broadly to suggest that his opponents are subhuman. "Should I not also have the right to eliminate millions of an inferior race that multiplies like vermin?" Hitler said, "The rats that poison our body-politic gnaw from the hearts and memories of the broad masses even that little which distress and misery have left." Hitler wrote in "Mein Kampf" according to a translation published by Project Gutenberg.

A 1939 report from a French official recalls Hitler and a Nazi official pressing the idea that "this vermin must be destroyed. The Jews are our sworn enemies." As Hitler historian Max Domarus recalled in his book "The Essential Hitler." Hitler's argument for this monstrous crime was quite simple: Jews, like Russians, were not human. They were "animals and beasts." If valuable men had to die each day at the front, then it was really of no consequence if such vermin like the Jews were killed. They were no different from "tuberculosis bacilli." If such "innocent natural creatures as rabbits and deer" had to die, then why should "the beasts, who want to bring us Bolshevism, be spared?"

The idea that the German government was being haplessly overtaken by Marxists and those who must be rooted out — as Trump has suggested is happening in the United States — also coursed through Hitler's commentary.

"The German State is intensely overrun by Marxism," Hitler wrote in "Mein Kampf." He added at another point: "But there is one thing [Germany's leaders] have not known how to do, and that is how to save the German people from falling into the arms of Marxism. In that, they have shown themselves most pitiably and miserably impotent."

And at another: "What must be said of those State officials, chiefs of police, and even cabinet ministers, who showed a scandalous lack of principle in presenting themselves externally to the public as 'national' and yet shamelessly acted as the henchmen of the Marxists in the disputes which we, National Socialists, had with the latter."

And another: "We must overthrow Marxism so that for the future National Socialism will be master of the street, just as it will one day become master of the State."

Hitler also wrote about rooting out such forces.

"We must first root out the causes which led to our collapse and we must eliminate all those who are profiting by that collapse," he wrote.

Trump, like Hitler, even mentioned rooting out such forces *while* labelling them "vermin."

"It ought to have been the duty of any Government which had the care of the people in its keeping, to take this opportunity of mercilessly rooting out everything that was opposed to the national spirit," Hitler wrote in "*Mein Kampf*." "While the flower of the nation's manhood was dying at the front, there was time enough at home at least to exterminate this vermin."

"The threat from outside forces is far less sinister, dangerous and grave than the threat from within," Trump said Saturday. "Our threat is from within."

This was also a theme often promoted by Hitler.

"But we can see already how our racial peoples which are today still hostile to us will one day recognise the greater inner enemy," Hitler said in a January 1941 speech in Berlin, according to the Jewish Virtual Library. "For never in our history have we been conquered by the strength of our outside enemies but only through our failings and the enemy in our camp," he wrote in *Mein Kampf*

"Had they believed in what they did, they ought to have recognised that the strength of a nation lies, first of all, not in its arms but in its will, and that before conquering the external enemy the enemy at home would have to be eliminated," he also wrote.

Trump turned heads last month by upping his anti-immigrant rhetoric in a way that the New York Times likened to Hitler's rhetoric. "It is a very sad thing for our country," Trump said. "It's poisoning the blood of our country. It's so bad, and people are coming in with disease. People are coming in with every possible thing that you could have." Trump added during an Iowa rally: "It's the blood of our country; what they're doing is destroying our country."

Hitler in *Mein Kampf,* employing a more explicit construct, repeatedly cited the danger of German blood being poisoned by Jews and warned more broadly of how such a thing endangers a nation. "All the great civilisations of the past became decadent because the originally creative race died out, as a result of contamination of the blood," he wrote. "And so this poison was allowed to enter the national bloodstream and infect public life without the Government taking any effectual measures to master the course of the disease," he added. "He poisons the blood of others but preserves his blood unadulterated," Hitler wrote off the Jews. "It seemed as if some all-pervading poisonous fluid had been injected by some mysterious hand into the bloodstream of this once heroic body," he added.

In *Mein Kempf* Hitler even referred to the idea that Teutonic people in North America had been succeeding because they hadn't allowed their blood to be poisoned. "But in North America, the Teutonic element, which has kept its racial stock pure and did not mix it with any other racial stock, has come to dominate the American Continent and will remain master of it as long as that element does not fall a victim to the habit of adulterating its blood." Trump's language is similar.

CHAPTER 11

ONLY A PAWN IN THE GAME.

In the blistering heat of the later afternoon of Saturday 13th July 2024, tens of thousands of supporters of Republican nominee Donald Trump waited patiently at a rally in Butler, Pennsylvania. As he took the stage many wearing MAGA slogan" Make America Great Again" hats, cheered as he started his speech. He had hardly begun his rhetoric delivery when a volley of high-pitched gunfire came out. A bullet went through the upper left ear of the would-be second-term President and he ducked down and was quickly surrounded by Secret Service agents standing nearby. The young man who attempted the assassination had been shot dead moments before Trump was helped to his feet by secret service agents, as his blood poured from his upper ear and across his left cheek, he stood definitely with clenched fist raised calling out " Fight, fight, fight." It is an image that will be remembered long after the history of this event is written.

Nobody seems to know nor understand the young assassin's motivation it is some crazy reason or left-wing extremist viewpoint. No, at this point in the lead-up to the November election, it doesn't seem to be a worked-out plot to kill the man most likely to become the President again. There is nothing to indicate a plot and the young man who attempted to kill Trump was shot to death by the Secret Service

Sadly one member of the public was shot to death protecting his family at the rally and another two were seriously wounded. Some stipulate that if someone would want to stop The attempted assassination of Donald Trump has put pay to the Bidden campaign. The Democrats had an arsenal of adverts ready to launch into Donald Trump before Saturday's attempt on his life. Biden was thus convinced got step down in favour of Vice President Harris. His statement "There is nothing more sacred than our democracy but Donald Trump is ready to burn it all down." carried little weight as the attempted assassination put pay to the Biden campaign. And just two days before the shooting he accused Trump of being a poodle of Russia's war criminal President: " This is who Donald Trump is the United States must never be like Putin's Russia, we don't empower dictators." Two weeks before the shooting, former House speaker Nancy Pelosi declared on national television that: "This is not a normal election," and "Trump must be stopped, he cannot become president." Biden had repeated repeatedly "It's time we put Trump in the bullseye." He has since the shooting qualified that statement as he must be the target to beat and did not mean it to sound"in the crosshairs," but the damage was done.

The Democrats seem to believe they're history. What else short of violence don't they do to make Trump seem an evil that had to be stopped by hook or crook? For the past three years, Democrats have pushed the bogus claim that Trump stole the 2016 election by colluding with Russia. Then Democrats falsely accused Trump of sending a mob to invade Congress to stop Biden from replacing him as president. They even falsely accused Trump of " having sat and watched the cops being killed" when the only person killed was a female Trump supporter shot by police. This Trump Derangement Syndrome is just a slogan. It is a sick reality in the US that looks at time almost like a civil war. God knows what would have happened if Trump had been killed.

The Democrats even felt licensed to bend and strain the law to launch four separate legal cases to get Trump jailed or at least cripple his progress ahead of the November election. And the left media did their bit too. The New Republic last month ran a cover story with a Hitler likeness of Trump on the cover and a headline: " American fascism, what it would be like." Not to be outdone the American Prospect magazine, The New Yorker had a cover story with a Moustache Trump goose-stepping with the headline " Why we can't stop arguing about whether Trump is a fascist." And all the way the media accused Trump of saying:" Nazies are good people, and his plan to be dictator from day one." So can anyone be surprised when a wayward youth may have decided to remove him because of being told he is an evil monster? A Hitler?

The Democrat's attempt to co-opt the FBI into making Trump seem in collusion with Putin just made the Deep State look corrupt. The Democrats' attempt to stop the Trump campaign in the courts just made the h justice system look corrupt and gain him more support. And now the assassination attempt on his life will make Trump unbeatable in this election. Not just because of his courage under fire when he raised his fist in the air in front of the American flag shouting "fight, fight fight" It seems to the average American that there is an existing threat from within the current Government against peace and freedom of America.

There is speculation that Trump was (is) backed by the Palestine Jewish elite and the American military for his past term as President and present ambitious campaign to return to the White House in the November 2024 election. In April 2018 reporter Michael Salta wrote an article that Q-Anon, the military intelligence agent, had close connections with Trump. According to the veteran investigative reporter and best-selling author Dr. Jerome Coris, he was approached there years earlier by a group of generals and told that Donald Trump had been recruited by U.S. military intelligence to run in the 2016 Presidential elections, and subsequently helped remove corrupt " Deep State" officials (alleged secret network of especially non-elected government officials and private entities) from positions of power. Coris claims Q-Anon's far-right American conspiracy represents the same group of senior military intelligence officials who are exposed to Deep state corruption and officials involved in a history of treasonous actions against the U.S. Republic.

In an April 2018 interview with Alex Jones, founder of Info-Wars.com, Jerome Coris is reported to have stated "About three years ago a group of generals came to me, and it was explained to me that they were ready to conduct a Coup d'état. They were ready to remove Barack Obama from office with military force. Then a few weeks later I got another call and they were reconsidering. "Do you know why they were re-considering? " Because they talked to Donald Trump and Trump had agreed he would run, and they agreed that if he would run, they would conduct their coup d'état as a legitimate process, rooting out the traitors important to note that Corsi claims happened only a day after a tweet by President Trump about 20 senior U.S. military officials with whom he dined the previous night." Last night, it was my great honour to host America's senior defence and military leaders for dinner at the White House. America's military is the greatest fighting force in the history of the world. They all have my pledge of unwavering commitment to our men and women in uniform. One hour after Trump's tweet Q-Anon posted a photo with those present at the dinner. In the photo, the man next to Vice President Pence and Donald Trump was Admiral Michale Rogers, the head of the National Security Service.

In November 2016, a week after the election, Admiral Rogers met with Donald Trump at Trump Tower in New York without the knowledge of senior Defence and intelligence officials. The Washington Post reported a story that senior defence and intelligence officials in the Obama administration were against Rogers's action due to sensitive breach of anonymity issues of internal matters. The Washington Post went on to report that a recommendation had previously been made to President Obama to remove Rogers in October 2016 by James Capper, Director of National Intelligence, and Ashton Carter, the Secretary of Defence.

The Foreign Intelligence Service Court approved a request by President Obama for his administration to spy on the Trump campaign before the election. Given recent disclosures that the FISC approved the spying on Trump, it is not unreasonable to understand why Rogers travelled to New York to warn Trump about the intelligence community and who was spying on him. It would therefore be fair to conclude that QAnon acted with the approval or support of Admiral Rogers and that intelligence data was being anonymously leaked to expose the extent of the Deep State corruption in the White House by those opposed to Trump.

So the pact between Donald Trump and the military has held throughout Trump's first term. So from a military aspect, what did Trump achieve in aligning himself with the U.S. military from the word go? Well, it must be remembered that unlike every former President from George Washington to Barack Obama — there has never been a president who has entirely lacked both political and military service. Donald Trump has broken this barrier. He had no previous public service experience or time in the military. The previous US presidents (1789 to 2016) came into the White House with an average of 13 years in public office and 5.6 years of military service.

Trump's lack of public service is part of the "outsider" appeal that may have contributed to his success in his first term. The Pols of the day have shown that most Americans, especially Trump supporters, distrust the government. "[Trump], Thank God, is not a politician," one supporter tweeted back in March. "But he's one heck of a fighter who will fight for us, the people." So will that be so in his second term and what can be gleaned from his now from his four-year public service first term both economically in America and military wise internationally?

President Trump campaigned as a billionaire businessman and champion of the working class with the economic prowess and deal-cutting skills that politicians in Washington, D.C., lacked. He summed up his position neatly during the campaign: "I'll be the greatest jobs president that God ever created."

On the campaign trail, Trump claimed to be laser-focused on bringing back manufacturing and mining jobs, renegotiating trade deals that led to work disappearing overseas and curtailing immigration. His Clinton-like tack of "it's the economy, stupid," despite the myriad scandals and investigations that dogged him, largely worked as GDP grew at a healthy clip, the stock market soared and unemployment rates hit a half-century low until the coronavirus pandemic gutted the job market. Yet as he left after his one-term tenure, Trump became the first president since Herbert Hoover during the Great Depression to depart office with fewer jobs in the country than when he entered.

Donald Trump ended his term in office just as he started it: lying about being "anti-war." He had claimed without evidence that he had opposed the invasion of Iraq, and Trump lambasted the bipartisan foreign policy establishment for its decades of disastrous militarism. For a war-weary nation desperate for change, this was evidence enough that Trump would be different. The "anti-war" label stuck, and it would be repeated over and over, up to the very final days of his presidency. Donald Trump didn't launch a new all-out ground invasion on the scale of Iraq. But he did escalate the conflict in every theatre of war he inherited, repeatedly brought the country to the brink of new wars, and recklessly threw around U.S. power with no regard for the many lives it would cost. Trump's foreign policy was characterised above all by an aversion to diplomacy and a knee-jerk reliance on hostility. Attacking diplomatic relations and torpedoing successful multilateral agreements like the Iran nuclear deal, Trump instead tried to strong-arm other countries into doing his bidding through threatening rhetoric, military brinkmanship, and suffocating sanctions. The result? Not a single one of Trump's targets for hybrid warfare is any closer to doing his bidding now than when he started (often for the best). In the meantime, countless thousands have suffered the consequences.

Despite repeated PR stunts Trump did not "bring the troops home" or "end endless wars." Trump consistently added fuel to the fire, increasing troop levels, deepening reliance on private contractors, and dramatically scaling up aerial warfare. Where an end to endless war requires repealing the 2001 and 2002 Authorisations for Use of Military Force, Trump expanded conflicts under both. His term saw four consecutive years of growth of an already out-of-control Pentagon budget. And loosening even the minimal restrictions that were already in place, he expanded the United States' deadly and unaccountable drone wars. Not only did Trump not end the wars he promised to, but he worsened them, dropping more bombs, stroking further conflict, undermining the prospects of peace, and massively increasing the rate of civilian deaths.

U.S. support for the Saudi- and UAE-led intervention in the war in Yemen is one of the most egregious examples of destructive militarist foreign policymaking in years. Not only did Trump do nothing to end U.S. complicity himself, but he repeatedly used his veto power to override bipartisan majorities in Congress that tried to cease U.S. military involvement and block the flow of arms to the conflict.

Trump shredded the Intermediate-Range Nuclear Forces Treaty, withdrew from the Open Skies Treaty that ensured transparency between the U.S., much of Europe, and Russia, and failed to extend the critical New START Treaty with Russia. He took an inconsistent, self-serving, and often antagonistic approach to negotiations with North Korea that nearly took us to nuclear war. In short: the world is closer to nuclear war than it was before Trump took office.

And back home communities of colour peoples have suffered since well before Trump. But Trump took these wars even further, escalating Islamic phobia, terrorising migrants and asylum-seekers at the Southern border, violently repressing racial justice protesters, and so much more.

But these points are just the highlights. From selling weapons to dictators to trying to launch a new drone war in Kenya, to stoking a Cold War with China, the list of reasons Trump is undeserving of the "anti-war" title is endless. The roots of U.S. military violence extend far beyond Trump, but there can be no doubt: Donald Trump's foreign policy legacy is nothing but violence, suffering, and conflict.

Trump's undeserved label is attributable to a basic but insidious mistake. For decades, U.S. foreign policy has been motivated by the belief in a U.S.-underwritten world order: The United States would be the supreme global power. It would use its power to create a rules-based system of liberal capitalist global governance (though the United States itself would largely be exempt from those rules). It would then promote and protect this order by the barrel of a gun.

To commentators unable to see beyond this ideology, the fact that Trump would attack international institutions like NATO or the World Trade Organisation was evidence that he was rejecting the whole project, turning America inward toward "restraint" and "isolationism." In reality, while Trump denied the first half — eschewing internationalist cooperation or rulemaking he maintained the latter, continuing to use violent force abroad on a whim when he thought that it would be to the national benefit. In short, he was a national chauvinist, completely fine with military adventurism, but opposed to even a whiff of multilateralism.

But if the pre-Trump status quo means international engagement, Trump was never anti-war. Not when he was a candidate, and not after his first four years in office. But there's a reason his attacks on the pro-war establishment took hold. The people are still tired of the status quo. Americans still want change irrespective of the consequences. Donald Trump's addressing the United Nations in New York and threatening to "destroy" one of its member states, North Korea, was shocking but not surprising given the belligerence of his rhetoric.

To witness him describing the neo-Nazis who had marched with tiki torches in Charlottesville, Virginia, as "very fine people" could be described in the same terms because Trump had repeatedly failed to disavow his far-right supporters. Even the insurrection that Trump incited on January 6, 2021, fell under this rubric. The storming of the US Capitol, to prevent the certification of Joe Biden's clear-cut election victory, fitted a pattern of norm-busting and democracy denying. When he urged his supporters to " fight like hell ", MAGA diehards were prepared to act on this violent presidential directive.

The violence on January 6th was seen by many of its perpetrators as historically legitimate. Many of these insurrectionists chanted "1776", believing themselves to be American patriots acting in the spirit of the revolution.

Thomas Jefferson, the primary author of the Declaration of Independence, once said that the "tree of liberty must be refreshed from time to time with the blood of patriots and tyrants". Over the years, those words have become something of a far-right behaviour mindset and taken at face value.

Partisan rage has now become the defining characteristic of US politics, and it came to the fore immediately after the assassination attempt in Pennsylvania. This time it was Republicans who blamed Democrats for inciting violence through their demonisation of Donald Trump. The kind of attack that in another country might unify the nation ended up exposing its all too familiar fault lines. Minutes after the shooting, conspiracy theories also abounded on social media, that modern-day super-spreader of misinformation. Had the Secret Service allowed the attack to take place, given so many rally attendees had noticed the gunman lying on the roof? Had Joe Biden or the "deep state" ordered and orchestrated a hit? Had the Republicans staged the entire event? But, as with political violence and mass shootings, conspiracy-mongering has long been an American contagion.

The electoral ramifications of the failed assassination attempt are potentially immense. The image of Trump punching the air, and shouting "fight, fight, fight", with the stars and stripes fluttering above, became instantly iconographic. Often his supporters have borrowed warrior-like imagery, casting him as Rambo or the Terminator on their t-shirts and ensigns. But now many of his supporters are inking that dramatic image of his near martyrdom into their skin.

Trump's show of defiance after surviving his would-be assassin's bullets stands in glaring contrast to Biden's disastrous debate performance, which has stirred dismay within the Democratic Party. Indeed, just as Trump's fist pump has become the defining image of the 2024 election, Biden's fumbled answers have become its defining soundbites. So, for now, at least, the attempt on Trump's life has strengthened democrats' position when it comes to holding on to power, and now that Biden has bowed out of the race in favour of Vice President Kamila Harris who makes it be the winning of four years in the White House is more uncertain..

Nothing is preordained. A Trump restoration is not guaranteed. The race for the White House will see more twists and turns. But in this emphatically American moment, a convicted felon, who as president incited an insurrection, is the favourite to win one of the most consequential elections in US history. That may be shocking to his detractors, both in America and abroad, but surely few would find it surprising. What happened on Saturday, July 13th, then, is deeply rooted in American history, and follows the same perilous path the country has been travelling in for decades.

Assassination attempts and plots on the President of the United States have been numerous, ranging from the early 19th to the early 21st centuries. On January 30, 1835, Andrew Jackson was the first president to experience an assassination attempt when Richard Lawrence twice tried to shoot him in the East Portico of the Capitol after Jackson left a funeral held in the House of Representatives Chamber. The attempt failed when both of Lawrence's pistols misfired.

CHAPTER 12

O LIVE AND LET DIE

The gunfire attempt of Donald Trump by Thomas Matthew Crooks is the third of Presidents who have been injured in an attack. The first president to be shot at was Theodore Roosevelt in 1912 when John Schank attempted to kill the President. He later said he was not insane but that God had selected him to receive visions and that he was motivated to prevent Roosevelt from becoming a king. Authorities found papers in Schrank's possession that showed that he had been stalking Roosevelt for some time. It seems God was on Roosevelt's side as the assassin's bullet lodged in Roosevelt's chest after penetrating Roosevelt's steel eyeglass case and passing through a 50-page-thick (single-folded) copy of his speech titled "Progressive Cause Greater Than Any Individual", which he was carrying in his jacket pocket. Then the next was Ronald Reagan while in office in 1981 by John Hinckley Jr., He had no political motive: He had become obsessed with the actress Jodie Foster and thought he could impress her by shooting the president, just 18 years after President John F. Kennedy had been assassinated. **Reagan was seriously wounded but no last injuries resulted.**

There have been four sitting presidents who an assassin's bullet has killed. The first was Abraham Lincoln the actor and Southern supporting activist John William Booth set the President in 1865. Then in 1881 James A Garfield was shot by Charles J. Guiiteau, age thirty-nine at the time, who was known around Washington as an emotionally disturbed man. He had killed Garfield because the president had refused to appoint him to a European consulship.

Of all the assassinations of President John F. Kennedy the most unanswered reasons as to who did the killing are still uncertain. In 1961, reportedly by Lee Harvest Oswald is the most politically motivated and surrounded by controversy.

There are many documented assumptions as to the killing of JFK. His affiliation with The Mafia, suggestions of links to Nazism and the Catholic democratic establishment through his father's connections, his support of Civil Rights activists and the Black Power movement, and his efforts to control unions by legislation and stamp our secret societies. His speeches and actions in that regard cost him his life as they did his brother Bobby Kennedy the former Attorney General when JFK was in office. *

John F Kennedy born in the 20th century was one of the best educated, having graduated from Harvard cum laude. Whilst Cold War leaders in America could only see the dangers of Communism, Kennedy was the first to warn of the dangers of necessary secrecy and secret societies like the Skull and Bones, the Council of Foreign Relations and the political elite, the Bilderberg Group. Kennedy in a 1961 address to the American Newspaper Publishers Association. stated: " The very word ' secrecy' is repugnant in a free and open society, and we are as a people inherently and historically opposed to secret societies; to secret oaths, and secret proceedings." *

Kennedy had written two successful books before his bid for the presidency. The book that made him a public figure was the successful selling " Why England Slept", a pre-war epic of British-German diplomacy, that showed clearly Kennedy had a keen understanding not only of geopolitics but of the behind-the-scenes machinations of the globalists.

Interestingly is how his political career may have not got going for his relationship with an alleged Nazi spy. Early in World War 11, FBI agent J Edgar Hoover suspected a former Miss Denmark, a then-American foreign correspondent, of being a spy. Whilst in Germany she had attended Germany's Field Marshal Hermann Goering's wedding and had been in contact with Adolf Hitler. She was considered to be a Nazi spy after the FBI eavesdropped on her liaisons with a young Naval Ensign John F Kennedy, who was working for naval Intelligence in Washington at the time. Hoover of the FBI informed both the Navy and Joseph Kennedy, of the dangers presented by Kennedy's involvement with a suspected agent. It was not long after that young John F Kennedy was transferred to the South Pacific. It was as a Naval Captain in the Pacific on the PT 109 that he became a war hero and launched another book " PT 109": and his political career towards the presidency. Whilst J. Edgar Hoover was never trusted by the Kennedy brothers, it was thanks to his diligence that JFK became president. *

In 1960 Corporate heads and their Nazi backers were presumably mortified knowing that he was being guided by his father Joseph Kennedy and his pro-Nazi sympathisers. By Mid-1963, Kennedy was beginning to exert his influence over the most powerful and violent groups in U.S. society. He was to threaten to disband the C.I.A, the home base of many Nazis; withdraw troops from South Vietnam, close the tax-free foreign assets of oil depletion allowance, tighten control over the tax-free foreign assets of U.S. multinational corporations, many with connections to the Bormann en empire; a decrease the power of Wall Street capitalists and the federal Reserve system. In June 1963, Kennedy ordered the printing and release of $4.2 billion in US Notes, paper money issued through the Treasury Department without paying interest to the Federal Reserve System, which is composed of twelve regional banks all controlled by private banks whose owners often were non-Americans.

Those affected by these moves felt something had to be done. Most people agree that the assassination of President Kennedy was the result of conspiracy, the full details of which are still not known due to cover up at the highest levels of federal government.

The connections between Kennedy's death and the Nazi persona, shadow groups, and corporate firms, are well documented. The CIA, which had provided hundreds of millions of dollars to the secret Organisation, was fingered as a major player in the assassination. Operatives of the Watergate burglars, E. Howard Hunt and Frank Statgait, CIA's Desmond Futgerakdm, mobster Johnny Roselli, Cubin minister Dr. Rondo Cabela;'s defrocked New Orland's priest David Ferrie and anti-Castro Cubans Carlos

Bringuier, Orlando Boschm and Carlos Prio Soccatras all played roles in the CIA intelligence mix surrounding the assassination. There was George DelMohrenschilde, a Dallas oil geologist, later known to be a friend of accused assassin Lee Harvey Osward who began his intelligence career as a Nazi agent. He according to CIA documents had applied to work for US intelligence back in 1942 but was turned down because of his Nazi links. His cousin Baron Constantine Meydell was one of the top Nazi intelligence agents in North America and after the war was recruited into the Gehlen Organisation to direct CIA's Russian 'emigre' pro-gratis. At the time DeMohrenschildt was befriending Oswald in Dallas and introduced him to White Russian communities there. He was in close contact with his friend J. Walter Moore, an agent of the CIA's domestic Contracts Division. Oswald's other close associates at the time before the assassination were Ruth and Michael Paine. Oswald's wife was staying at the Paine home at the time of the assassination, and it was Ruth Paine, a woman with CIA connections, who got Oswald his job at the Texas Book Depository, the location where he reportedly shot JFK. Oswald had claimed to Dallas police- who found incriminating photos of Oswald holding a rifle in Paine's garage- that the photo had been fabricated.*

Michael Paine had worked for Bell Aerospace Corporation in Texas when his boss was Bell aircraft director of research and development and research has proven him to be the notorious war criminal General Walter Dornberger. Oswald's connections to the CIA are documented - his training in Japan's Atsugi base, which housed a large CIA facility, his incredible ability to speak fluent Russian despite lack of evidence of language lessons, testimony of his employment by fellow marines and a former CIA paymaster, also confirmed his ease in obtaining a U.S. passport, his daily diary entries and his possession of a miniature Minox "spy" cameras with a serial number proving it was not commercially available in America at the time provides a suspicion he was involved in the plot to assassination to kill the president. *

The most often pointed evidence involving both Nazi mentality and actual Nazis in Kennedy's assassination can be found in a treatise passed around for years under the name of " Torbitt document." This document first appeared under the pen name of William Torbitt but was written by a Texas attorney named David Copeland, who verified that he had received the information from friends in both the FBI and the Secret Service, Based on this information, Copeland spent considerable effort searching for evidence to support the documents thesis.

According to the 'Torbitt Document': Kennedy's assassination was orchestrated through a nexus of Nazi-infiltrated anti-communist organisations, elements of the military-industrial complex, the CIA, and the FBI. Torbiant explained: "The director of the FBI was in charge of NASA's Security Division and the Defence Industrial Security Command, the DISC, in his position as head of counterespionage activities in the United States. Torbitt reported that NASA security personnel who were assigned duties in connection with the assassination and were employees or contractors for Division Five of the FBI. " it must be said that it was a relatively small group with the agency. It was not official, not an American operation, but simply the independent action taken by those men, some of what happened to hold official positions." he wrote. *

Torbirt's tale of a NASA conspiracy was supported by New Orleans District Attorney Jim Garrison, who was investigating Kennedy's assassination. In 1958 Garrison telephoned magazine editor Warren Hinkle to say: "Important new evidence has surfaced. Those Texas oilmen do not appear to have been involved in Kennedy's murder in the way it was first thought. It was the military-industrial complex that put up the money for the assassination as far as we can tell, the conspiracy was limited to the Aerospace wing of NASA. We've got the names of three companies and their employees who were involved in setting up the president's murder."

When Garrison attempted to subpoena the testimony NASA refused to provide them, citing reasons of national security. Amazing enough accused assassin Lee Harvey Oswald told garage owner Adrian Alba that he soon expected to work in a New Orleans plant of NASA. Why Oswald had tried to defect to Russia and voiced hostility towards the USA and its policies, then thought he could go work for a US aerospace agency was never explained.

According to the Torbitt document, this complex matrix of government agencies, and NASA employees, was a Nazi-managed assignment by Louis Moeine Bloomfield of Montreal, Canada. Bloomfield was an ardent Zionist, an attorney, businessman, and philanthropist who had worked for OSS during World War 11, and for the fledgling CIA. Torbitt stated Bloomfield was a longtime friend and confidant of J. Edgar Hoover and had been Hoover's contact supervisor of Division Five since his days in the SS before World War 11. According to Torbitt "Bloomfield was the coordinator of all activities, responsible only to Hoover and Johnson in carrying out the plans for John Kennedy's assassination." *

In 1967 New Orleans DA Jim Garrison charged Clay Shaw, a former OSS officer and founder of the city's International Trade Mart, with conspiracy to assassinate the president. According to several separate sources- Garrison's files and an investigation by the US Labor Party- the International Trade Mart in New Orleans was a subsidiary of a shadowy entity known as the Centro Mondiale Commerciale (CMC) or World Trade Centre, which was founded by Bloomfield in Montreal in the late 1950s, then moved to Rome in 1961. The Trade Mart was connected with the CMC through another firm known as Permindex, also in the business of international expositions. According to Torbitt, Bloomfield held half of the shares of Penmindex and was in total command of its operation in Europe and Africa, as well as North and South American countries. Whatever the truth may be CMCV and its companion company Permindex were connected to Kennedy's assassination. The government saw fit to expel both firms in 1962 for the subversive activities identical to those in the much-publicised Propaganda -2 (P 2) Masonic Lodge Scandal of the Reagan years. *

Today it is clear that Clay Shaw was tightly connected to the CIA and intelligence work despite his denials at the time of the Garrison investigation. It is interesting to note that while serving in the U.S. Army during World War 11, Shaw worked as aide-de-camp to General Charles O. Thrasher and as a liaison officer to the headquarters of Winston Churchill. At the time of his arrest by Garrison, Shaw's personal address book was taken. It revealed the names and contact information of important Europeans, many of them being pro-Nazi royalty or Bilderberg members. *

Another odd connection was SS Oberfruppenfueher Karl Wolff who had headed the Gestapo in Italy. As part of Allen Dulle's hide-the-Nazi program, Wolff was sentenced to four years imprisonment after the war but served only a week. By 1983 Wolff and some SS associates gathered in Hamburg on Herman Goring's former yacht, Corin11. The boat then belonged to Goring's widow, Emmy, whose estate attorney was the celebrated Melvin Belli. He had represented the Nazi-connected actor Errol Flynn, as well as Jack Ruby, the man who shot Lee Harvey Oswald. *

In a letter smuggled out of Dallas County jail and brought to the attention of JFK examination researcher Penn Jones, written by Oswald's killer Jack Ruby, it stated: "My time is running out… they plan on doing away with me" Ruby pointed to Lyndon Johnson as one of those behind Kennedy's assassination. He had added '… certain powers would have questions to find the truth about me before he would relinquish certain powers to these certain people… Consequently, a whole new form of government is going to take over our country and I know I won't be alive to see you another time."   After advising a friend to read his letter J. Evers Haley's noted blistering remarks regarding 'certain people and comments by Ruby: "This man LBJ, is a Nazi in the worse order." * It was less than two hours after JFK was shot that J Edgar Hoover wrote: " I called the attorney general at his home and told him I thought we had the man that killed the president down in Dallas."   FBI documents released in 1977 stated that

Hoover at the time had told Lyndon Johnson's aide Walter Jenkins; " the thing I am concerned about is having something issued so we can convince the public that Oswald is the real assassin." *

An insightful view of the JFK assassination comes from inside information of Nazi SS officer Otto Skoraeny, who had served time with the CIA and under former Director George H. W. Bush. He had been quoted as saying:" One of the worst kept secrets in the CIA, is the truth about the president's murder. It wasn't Castro or the Russians. The men who killed Mr. Kennedy were CIA contract agents. John Kennedy's murder was a two-part conspiracy murder. One was the action ending with the killers, the other was the deeper part, the acceptance and protection of that murder by the intelligence apparatus that controls the way the world operates. It had to happen. The man was too independent for his good."

It is well apparent that the killing was not solely by German Nazis. But as previously reported, men with Nazi connections- before, during and after World War 11. Men who were also members of secret societies, who were most opposed to Kennedy's policies. They had the power and influence to affect such an assassination and certainly were capable of blocking any meaningful investigation- either by the government or the media right up to the present day.

Interestingly the men most closely involved in the Warren Commission investigation of JFKs death were John J. McCloy and Allen Dalles, both men with close Nazi connections, along with Gerald R. Ford, who was spying on the commission for J. Edgar Hoover. It was noted by Professor Donald Gibson of the University of Pittsburg that " both of these men [McCloy and Dalles] had always been the Establishment men in government, and they were the government's men in the Establishment too." When McCloy served as high commissioner in Germany as president of the World Bank or as a member of the so-called Warren Commission, he did so as a servant of the ruling elite. His most extensive ties were to various Rockefeller family interests. His long-term leading figure on the Warren Commission Allen Dalles, was also a man of the Establishment, even though his name is also associated with the CIA.*

Within days of Kennedy's death, the same forces opposing his policies began to propagate the official theory for his death- a lone assassin suffering a 'strain of madness and violence" fired at the president from the sixth floor of a book warehouse, striking him twice out of three shots fired within six seconds. This was even though the target was 265 feet, 80.7 metres away, moving laterally and downhill away from the shooter and an evergreen tree obscured the line sight of fire.

Within days of the shooting Alan Belmont of the FBI was pushing the Oswald did it alone conclusions and shortly thereafter McCloy and Dales were settling the dust with the same conclusions. The venue for the McClay-Dalles work was the Warren Commission created at the instigation of Establishment peoples within government. "The cover-up was essentially an operation of power based in the East Coast Establishment' Gibson concluded, adding the Warren commission was ' essentially an Establishment cover-up. Only an Establishment network could reach into the media, the CIA, and the FBI, the military had control over JFK's autopsy, and other areas of government.

As has been seen here, the inner core of the U.S. establishment was filled at the time with National Socialism, just as they had supported communism before that. "This global elite was working to lay the groundwork for the New World Order- worldwide socialism broken into three economic blocs to be o played against each other for profit and control.

So it is with the assassination of 1963 and the subsequent cover-up, that the globalists who first created communism and then National Socialism, had finally gained a new empire, A Fourth Reich. Only this time it is in North America.*

CHAPTER 13.

THE BANKERS BEHIND THE THRONE

When the 20th century dawned one hundred initial members of the Free-Masons were the ones who set the pathway of financial control standards by which the world still lives. This story of modern-day banking begins with the seed of the family tree, the essence of which flowed through generations of a German banking dynasty.

The first of the non-elite Jewish members to join a secret society on a mission to implement a One World Order was a German. He had been invited by those men who had royal blood links in both Europe and Britain which included politicians, and businessmen of financial influence but all of Jewish extraction at the time. In the late 18th Century on the Judengasse, a Jewish street, Frankfurt-on-Main, in Southern Germany the residence of Amschel Mayer, a Jew, and his wife, Gutta Schnapper. It was a wooden hut, imitating a gothic design with a first-floor residence in which they lived and it had a shop, where they bought and sold merchandise.

The little shop remains historically the birthplace of today's proud "Baron," the title of honour of the rulers of the world. Amschel and his wife were founding members of the Dynasty of a Secret Supreme World of Emperors and elite business associates. Amschel was to rise to the title of the leader of the World of finance. As family founder Amschel Meyer was a coin dealer in Frankfurt, a specialist in antique coins, who became the family's first banker. The Rothschild name originated in the red sign (in German, *rot schild*) that hung above the door of the family home in the Frankfurt ghetto in the mid-1700s; it eventually became part of the family's crest. Mayer Amshel adopted the sign as both the name of the family and the symbol of power for his part in the secret society of what was to become the Masonic One World Order.

The Rothschild family trace their origins back to 15th century Frankfurt. The ancestry of the Rothschild name can be traced back to 1577 to Izaak Elchanan Rothschild, whose name derived from the house he occupied in the Frankfurt Judengasse zum roten Schild ("at the sign of the red shield"). His grandchildren and descendants took this name as the family name and kept it when they relocated in 1664 to another house in the Judengasse which became the family's home and centre of business until the early 19th century.

Amsted was destined to become a rabbi and entered a school, which was the catalyst for his misrepresentation of Jewish Holy scriptures and the poisonous hatred he developed against Christians, which was instilled in him from an early age. Much like modern-day IS Islamic terrorism, the scriptures were interfered out of context by his rabbi, focusing on the Jihad-like interpretation of the Muslim text of the Arabic Qur'an, misinterpreting the fight against the perceived enemies of Islam. The true meaning of Jihad was and is of a different kind; a believer's internal struggle to live out the Muslim faith as well as possible. Similarly, The Jewish holy doctrine is the Talmud comprised of two parts, the first, the Mishnah written around 200 CE is a compendium of Rabbinic Judaism oral teachings of the Torah and the German, written around 500 CE Like a jihad interpretation, it is not difficult to read the content out of misunderstanding. In the broad Church reality, the Talmud, The Torah, The Qur'an, the Bible, as well as the New Testament parts of the Bible relating to the teachings of Christ, are there to help the followers to spiritual fulfilment.

Amschel, at the end of his biblical teaching, was sent to the Bank of Oppenheim at Hanover, where he remained for three years to serve as an apprentice. There he made the acquaintance of Lieutenant-General-General Baron von Estorff, the man nearest to Landgrave, Frederick11 of the Hesse Cassel. Returning to Frankfort in 1770 Amschel married Gutta Schnapper, raised five sons and five daughters and there they started their very modest business. Gutta looked after the shop and Amschel went around town with a trunk full of goods, to visit Jewish patriots and to inform himself. Soon, Amschel rendered some service to Baron von Estorff, at the expense of the bank of Oppenheim, and was introduced to the young Jew, titled Frederic 11, whose fortune was valued at around 100 million florins, a sum that was unheard of in those times.

Mayer Amschel Rothschild was born in the Hinterpfann in the Judengasse, one of eight children of Amschel Moses Rothschild (d. 1755) and his wife Schönche Rothschild (née Lechnich, d. 1756). He lived there throughout his childhood and much of his married life, until, in 1784, together with his wife Guile and their first five children, he was able to buy a larger house in the Judengasse; this property was known as the 'House at the Green Shield'. It was here that Mayer and Guile's ten children grew up, their five sons to become the future bankers to European monarchs and governments.

The five sons of Mayer Amschel Rothschild were placed on the first rung of the nobility by the Austrian Emperor in 1817. They were granted the right to heraldry bearings, and to use the suffix 'von' in their names. Those members of the family living in Frankfurt and Vienna were thus known as von Rothschild, whereas the Paris, and later the Naples, branches of the family adapted this to the French style 'de'. In England, Nathan Mayer Rothschild eschewed 'foreign' titles, and is reputed to have declared that *"plain Mr Rothschild"* was good enough for him. A letter in the Archive from Amschel to Salomon and Nathan in November 1816 reads, *".....James and Carl received the nobility. It is a pity that Nathan did not want it."* Nathan's sons thought differently, and in 1818 successfully applied to the Austrian title, using the French style 'de' rather than the German one.

In 1822 the Rothschild brothers were awarded an Austrian Barony granted by Imperial Decree. The Barony was granted to the five brothers and their heirs and descendants of both sexes. The design for the arms was modified at this stage to include a seven-pointed coronet, and there were five arrows, the lion and unicorn as supporters, three helmets and a Latin motto: 'Concordia, Integritas, Industria' (Harmony, Integrity, Industry).

The five arrows became an enduring symbol of the Rothschild name. The story comes from ancient Chinese myth and also is told by Plutarch of a wealthy man who, on his deathbed, asked his sons to break a bundle of darts. When they all failed, he showed them how easily the arrows could be broken individually, cautioning them that their strength as a family lay in their unity.

Many members of the Rothschild family began to adopt the motif on letterheads, bookplates, porcelain, and jewellery. Some individuals preferred to see the arrows pointing upwards, despite the official description of the arrows approved by the Austrian heralds of arms. Although this was purely a matter of personal choice, a cross-channel split of opinion began to develop. The French family and bank gradually adopted 'arrows up' for all uses of the symbol, while the English remained faithful to the 'arrows down' version.

The Rothschild banking dynasty originates with Mayer Amschel Rothschild, a rare coin dealer born in 1744 who advised German aristocrats on their finances. He sent his five sons to major European cities to do business with cash-strapped governments, and Nathan Mayer Rothschild was the first to venture abroad when he arrived on English shores at the end of the 18th century. Amschel's father had a business in goods trading and currency exchange. He was a personal supplier of collectable coins to the Prince of Hesse.

With the help of relatives, Amschel secured an apprenticeship under Jacob Wolf Oppenheimer, at the banking firm of Simon Wolf Oppenheimer in Hanover, in 1757. The grandson of Samuel Oppenheimer taught Amschel Rothschild useful knowledge of foreign trade and currency exchange before he returned to his brothers' business in Frankfurt in 1763. He became a dealer in rare coins and won the patronage of Crown Prince Wilhelm of Hesse (who had also earlier patronised his father). His coin business grew to include several princely patrons and then expanded through the provision of financial services to Crown Prince Wilhelm. In 1769, Mayer Amschel gained the title of "Court Agent", managing the finances of the immensely wealthy Elector of Hesse-Cassel who became Wilhelm IX, Landgrave of Hesse-Kassel in 1785. The business expanded rapidly following the French Revolution when Rothschild handled payments from Britain for the hire of Hessian mercenaries.

By the early years of the 19th century, Rothschild had consolidated his position as principal international banker to Wilhelm IX and began to issue his international loans, borrowing capital from the Landgrave. In 1806, Napoleon invaded Hesse in response to Wilhelm's support for Prussia. The Landgrave went into exile in the Duchy of Holstein, but Rothschild was able to continue as his banker, investing funds in London. He also profited from importing goods in circumvention of Napoleon's continental blockade. As a result of these dealings, Mayer Amschel amassed a not inconsiderable fortune and, in 1810, renamed his firm M A Rothschild und Söhne, establishing a partnership with his four sons still in Frankfurt, (his son Nathan Mayer Rothschild (1777-1836) having already established a business in Manchester and London).

Mayer Amschel Rothschild died on 19 September 1812 in Frankfurt am Main. He was buried at the old Jewish cemetery in Frankfurt, located next to the Judengasse. A park was named after him, and also a street (Rothschildallee). In 1817 he was posthumously ennobled by the emperor Francis I of Austria.

Jakob, Salomon, and Karl—the founders of the Rothschild consortium—were themselves unequally endowed: Nathan and Jakob stood out among their brothers by the force of their personalities—particularly Nathan, who was hard, deliberately boorish, and sarcastic. Jakob, who was his brother's equal in all these things, possessed an alleviating air of some refinement as a result of living in the more polished atmosphere of Paris. The five founders in turn had unequal successors. For example, if Alphonse in Paris (1827–1905) was a worthy successor to his father, Jakob, his son, Édouard (1868–1949), was not as strong a figure as his position required. But Édouard's son (Guy [1909–2007]) and his cousins (Alain [1910–82] and Elie [1917–2007]) showed exceptional adaptability and ambition, thus confirming the constant element in the group's history for a century and a half: a remarkable capacity for seizing opportunities and for adapting in business as well as in politics. Successive generations of the Rothschild family have been similarly active in international finance and politics.

In separating the circumstantial from the personal and individual aspects of the dynasty's hegemony during the 19th century, one must note that, although the first group of Rothschilds arrived as strangers in their new countries, unfamiliar with the languages and the customs and subject to the jealousy and competition of local bankers, they stood out from those around them by their fierce will to acquire a place in the sun. By the second generation, when the sons of the five founding brothers (notable among them were Anthony and Lionel Nathan in London and Alphonse and Gustave in Paris) entered the business, the Rothschilds were polished and refined, as well as naturalised to the point of blending into leadership positions without losing any of their family attributes. It is possible that the young Rothschilds' education and the extremely worldly existence of the heads of the various houses helped to create this true mutation. On the other hand, the Rothschilds were influencing the national economy and politics of their countries as greatly as they were being influenced themselves. Alphonse, for example, as the head of the international banking syndicate that in 1871 and 1872 placed the two great French loans known as liberation loans after France's defeat by

Prussia, could boast without immodesty that his influence had maintained the chief of the French government, Adolphe Thiers, in power. At the same time, in 1875, Lionel, in London (where he had been a member of the House of Commons since 1858), was able to give on a few hours' notice the £4 million that allowed the British government to become the principal stockholder in the Suez Canal Company the two cousins had become important citizens in their respective countries.

The Rothschild family is one of the most famous and influential in history. Their story begins in the late 18th century, with Amschels' banking business in Frankfurt, Germany. His five sons would later spread across Europe. Each son set up a bank in a different city: London, Paris, Vienna, Naples, and Frankfurt. This network allowed them to share information quickly. They could move money and resources with ease. The family became known for their wealth and power. They financed governments, supported industries, and invested in infrastructure. They played a key role in many historical events. Wars, peace treaties, and economic policies often saw their involvement. Their influence was both admired and criticised. Some saw them as visionaries, others as power-hungry. Their business practices were innovative. They used new methods to transfer money. They created a system of bonds that many countries adopted. They also invested in railways, mines, and other industries. Their success was due to their ability to adapt. They saw opportunities where others did not.

The Rothschild like so many other Jewish bankers is accredited as being a member of a "New World Order" a present-day brand for the masonic secrets society of the 19th century. There is no proof of their links with terrorists, assassins and funding criminal activity. Conspiracy theories postulate a global elite is trying to implement a single world government, and claim this is being achieved through manufactured crises, with the COVID-19 pandemic seen as one such man-made attempt to exert undue control over civilians. Anti-Masonic, anti-Illuminati and other theories that similarly posited the existence of an elite, "shadow" establishment date back to the 1800s. The foundations of the "New World Order" conspiracy as it is known today date to the mid-1900s, amid a rise in anti-globalist sentiment across the US. It is believed that they have funded governments, wars and corruption with the sole aim of the elite controlling mankind for the future. It may or may not be true but it is well documented that the Rothschilds are also known for their philanthropy. They supported education, arts, and science. They built schools, funded research, and collected art. Their legacy includes many institutions that still exist today. They believed in giving back to society.

CHAPTER 14.

A REPEAT OF HISTORICAL DICTATORSHIPS

At the time of Adolf Hitler's dictatorship, there were two other dictators of ruthless persuasion. One Benito Mussolini was instrumental in the rise of the Fascism movement, which galvanised as a growing nationalist movement in Europe born in the face of the First World War and the Bolshevik Revolution of 1917, in which Russian socialists overthrew the Russian Empire.

It was in Italy, that Mussolini led the way to fascism. Born on July 29, 1883, in small-town southern Italy to a blacksmith father and a schoolteacher mother, he grew up on his socialist father's stories of nationalism and political heroism. Shy and socially awkward, he ran into trouble at an early age due to his intransigence and violence against his classmates. As a young adult, he moved to Switzerland and became an avowed socialist. Eventually, he made his way back to Italy and established himself as a socialist journalist.

In protest, the prime minister and his cabinet resigned on the morning of October 28. So armed with a telegram from the king inviting him to form a cabinet, Mussolini boarded a sleeper car and took a leisurely 14-hour journey from Milan to Rome. On October 30, he became prime minister—and ordered his men to parade before the king's residence as they left the city. The king, exhausted by the world war and a state of near civil war in Italy, had assumed Mussolini would impose order. But within three years, the strongman would be an outright dictator—and Victor Emmanuel 111 King of Italy let him do as he pleased.

Over the years, Mussolini increased his power while chipping away at the population's civil rights and forming a propagandistic police state. His agenda also went beyond domestic affairs. Mussolini's imperial ambitions led Italy to occupy the Greek island of Corfu, invade Ethiopia, and ally itself with Nazi Germany, eventually resulting in the murder of 8,500 Italians in the Holocaust.

Mussolini's ambition would be his downfall. Though he led Italy into World War II as an Axis power aligned with the seemingly unstoppable Adolf Hitler, he presided over the destruction of much of his country. Victor Emmanuel III convinced Mussolini's closest allies to turn against him and, on July 25, 1943, they finally succeeded in removing him from power and placing him under arrest. After a dramatic prison break, Mussolini fled to German-occupied Italy, where, under pressure from Hitler, he formed a weak and short-lived puppet state. On April 28, 1945, as an Allied victory neared, Mussolini attempted to flee the country. He was intercepted by communist partisans, who shot him and dumped his body in a public square in Milan.

Another equally ruthless dictator that powered the Soviet Union, at the time was Joseph Stalin. He like Hitler called his adversaries "enemies of the state", before killing an estimated 750,000 during 1937's Greta Purge, while in the same year's legislative election, his Communist Party won 99 per cent of the vote. Stalin started his career as a robber, gangster as well as an influential member and eventually the leader of the Bolshevik faction of the Russian Social Democrat Party later to become known as the Communist Party. He served as the General Secretary of the Party, ruling the Soviet Union for more than 30 years, ruthlessly clamping down on dissents by sending millions of his adversaries to their deaths.

In 1917 two events changed Russia's future forever: the overthrow of the imperial government in February, followed by the Bolsheviks' rise to power in October and November. These events resulted in deteriorating relations between the vast majority of the people of Russia and the Tsar. They did not like his taking full control over the army in WW1 as opposed to letting his generals make strategic decisions. Russia suffered overwhelming casualties under the Tsar's leadership. The war also caused great economic loss for Russia and the people were suffering and desperate for change. Tsar Nicholas was forced to renounce his throne and a provisional government was put in place. It was not long after that He and his family were executed.

From October to November 1917, the Bolsheviks and Left Socialist Revolutionaries staged a coup. Behind the scenes during the Russian Revolution, the most avid spokesman was Vladimir Lenin. In his writings, he called for the Bolsheviks to halt their support of the Provisional government. He called for the party to come together with peasants, workers, and soldiers, thus uniting the Society against the government. The Party's slogan became " All Power to the Soviets." The Bolshevik wing of the Russian Social democratic Workers Party ad gained a monopoly over the entire political system in 1917. The Bolsheviks twice before WW11: The Russian Communist Party, and then the ALL-Union Communist Party. Still, the ideology remained the same.

Joseph Stalin became a dedicated follower of Lenin. In 1912 Lenin prompted Stalin to serve on the Central Committee of the Bolshevik Party. He also became editor of the Bolshevik newspaper *Provdo* before being exiled from July 1913 to March 1917 for political reasons. Stalin was involved in the October Revolution, but not as much as he would claim to have been in later years. Stalin became the most prominent figure when he became Secretary General of the Central Committee, even though he strong-armed his way into the position.

Tasked with raising money, Stalin resorted to criminal activity and took a leading role in the planning and execution of the 1907 Tiflis bank robbery. Before his exiled to Siberia from 1913 to 1917 he was one of the Bolshevik operatives in the Caucasus, organising cells, spreading propaganda, and raising money through criminal activities. Stalin also formed the Outfit, a criminal gang that was involved in armed robbery, racketeering, assassinations, arms procurement and using child couriers to transport goods and documents. His modus operandi was not unlike Hitler's Nazies as they rose to power. Stalin socialised with hitmen "Kamo and Tsintsadze" but issued formal commands to the rest of the Outfit members through his bodyguard Montefiore who also described Stalin during this formative period as a " terrorist gangster" in the Gulag. Stalin eventually earned a place in Lenin's inner circle and the highest echelons of the Bolshevik hierarchy. His pseudonym, Stalin, means "man of the steel hand".

Stalin forged connections with various Red Army generals and eventually acquired military powers of his own. He brutally suppressed counter-revolutionaries and bandits. After winning the Civil War, the Bolsheviks moved to expand the Revolution into Europe, starting with Poland, which was fighting the Red Army in Ukraine. Stalin, as joint commander of an army in Ukraine and later in Poland itself had the upper hand in policies of mass murder and suppression of opponents of which historical records estimate he killed over a million. In sham elections, the Communist Party won by supermajorities, portraying Stalin as the only unopposed leader who could rival the West. By 1928 Stalin drifted from Lenin's economic ideals to more state-organised fascist industrialisation. Stalin by definition had become a dictator. His reign consisted of femininity and genocide. Despite the crimes committed against his people, the Soviet Union was one of the chief Allied powers, along with Greta Britain and the United States, helping to thwart the rise of Nazi Germany during the Second World War.

Joseph Stalin, the second leader of the Soviet Union, died on 5 March 1953 at his Kuntsevo, Dacha district in Moscow, after suffering a stroke, at age 74. He was given a state funeral in Moscow on 9 March, with four days of national mourning declared. His body was embalmed and interred in Lenin's Mausoleum until 1961 when it was moved to the Kremlin Wall Necropolis. So there lay the most ruthless dictator of the 20th century not discounting the atrocities of Hitler's Jewish concentration camps and Mussolini being accused of killing thousands of Italians during the Holocaust.

Fast forward to the 21st century and the dictatorial leadership of Russia today. Putin grew up in Soviet Russia, rising through the ranks to become a KGB officer. Experts say that during his tenure as President from 2000 to 2008 and since 2012, he has exploited historical grievances surrounding the fall of the Soviet empire, which he has blamed on the West. The 71-year-old leader who was prime minister from 1999-2000 and 2008-2012, meaning he has been in power for 25 years is believed to have killed at least 20 political opponents, while state propaganda allows Putin to tighten his iron grip on the country.

But analysts say that while both are ruthless dictators, what Putin has done is incomparable to the scale of terror inflicted by Stalin. Marc Berenson, a senior lecturer in politics at King's College London, stated: "Putin may very well be as ruthless as the most brutal dictators the world has ever known, and this includes Stalin. However, today's world is not the same as the Soviet Union's 30s and 40s. Stalin may well have been responsible for tens of millions of Russian deaths, both directly and indirectly, whereas Putin still needs more time to catch up to that." While Putin should not be exonerated for his undoubted crimes, he is a " smaller man" than Stalin, Mark Galeotti, author of *Putin's Wars: from Chechnya to Ukraine*, wrote for this news outlet after Sunday's result. Putin as President-elect won 88% of the vote, the highest ever for a Russian election. The Constitution was amended in 2020 to reset the number of terms Putin has served, allowing him to circumvent term limits in the 2024 and 2030 elections, enabling him to legally stay in office until 2036

According to the Kyiv Independent newspaper, Putin has killed 20 political opponents since he rose to power in 1999. On the hit list were progressive opponents like Alexwi Navalyn, who died suddenly while out walking, warlord Yevgeny Prigozhin who threatened to march on Moscow before his plane mysteriously crashed, and Alexander Litvinenko, a former FSB officer critical of Putin who was then poisoned. The Kremlin denied involvement in the murders, while Putin called their deaths a "tragedy" or a "sad event".

If modern-day Russia were a democracy, Putin would have been unable to stand for re-election after 2008, when his second presidential term expired until he helped change the constitution. Sixteen years later, Russia's only independent election-monitoring organisation was designated by the Kremlin as a "foreign agent" and its co-founder thrown in jail. With prying eyes covered, experts said Putin was able to inflate his majority by approximately 30 million votes, allowing him to win the election by a fraudulent 88 per cent. If Putin can see out the next six years as President, he will have been in power as long as Stalin.

Sham elections in Russia serve an important purpose for Putin. While in the West, majorities of 88 per cent appear ludicrous, in states that have democratically backslid into authoritarianism, supermajorities serve to fend off opposition from elites, according to Dr Sean Roberts, a senior lecturer in politics at the University of Winchester and expert in Russian foreign policy

As in the days when Stalin purged the "elites", Putin's threat also comes from within the Russian state. David Lewis, Professor of Global Politics at the University of Exeter, stated: "The biggest threat comes not from the street or the diaspora, but from within the elite as we saw with Prigozhin's rebellion.

"This could emerge because of disputes over assets and business if the economy starts to fail, or over the potential succession to Putin – or maybe because a major defeat in the war with Ukraine sparks discontent in the military or security services. But at the moment, there is no real sign of any fracture in the elite – but we might not see evidence of internal discontent until it comes out in the open."

Meanwhile, approximately 1000 of Putin's political opponents are in prison. While they are no longer sent to the Gulag, many live in solitary confinement, banished to Siberian prisons for speaking out against Putin's reign. British-Russian political activist and former journalist Vladimir Kara-Murza was recently sentenced to 25 years in prison by a Russian court for "high treason" and other politically motivated charges for speaking out against Russia's invasion of Ukraine.

Dr Maxim Alyukov, a Russian political sociologist at Kings College London, said in an independent statement that the killings and imprisoning of opposition has left Putin with no organised opposition in Russia, as they have all been "completely demolished, killed or imprisoned."

When Nikita Khrushchev came to power after the death of Stalin, he denounced the dictator and his political repression in his "Secret Speech" of 1956, "On the Cult of Personality and Its Consequences". This followed a period of "De-Stalinisation", which saw statues of Stalin toppled and his reign condemned by the incumbent Soviet leadership.

Before his death, in 2022 opposition leader Navalny had described his sentence by Putin's government as "Stalinist". Murdering the Kremlin critic a month before his sham election was Putin's way of sending a message to anyone planning to oppose his rule in the years to come. But despite the killing and imprisoning of opposition leaders, people laid flowers on Navalny's grave and others spoke out against Putin as they invoked the dissident during Sunday's election.

Twenty years ago, a string of coincidences nearly set off a US-Russian nuclear crisis, but calmer heads prevailed. The risk is much higher today. In the different political circumstances of today, the same assessment of the Operational Deployment Force rocket's trajectory by Russia's political and military leaders might not be possible. Russia annexed Crimea, interfered in eastern Ukraine, and embarked on a major modernisation of its conventional forces. The United States and the North Atlantic Treaty Organisation have responded with sanctions, which, together with a precipitous fall in the price of oil, are destabilising the Russian economy and threatening President Vladimir Putin's popularity.

By way of counterbalance, the Middle East oil Kings are driving oil prices up for their mischievous ends. Russia has responded by cancelling the groundbreaking 1991 'cooperative threat reduction' program. One needs to consider the mind of Putin during his first term as the Leader of Russia to take a balanced stance on the likely outcome of Russia ahead in the risky darkness of nuclear war. A glance back in history to his rise to power and events that surrounded his first term in the Kremlin as a juxtaposition to his new wave of advancing Russia into this current age is worthy of consideration.

As a teenager, Putin was captivated by the novel and film series 'The Shield and the Sword.' The story focuses on a brave Soviet secret agent who thwarts the Nazis. Putin later said he was struck by how 'one spy could decide the fate of thousands of people.' It is the Apostle of the dark one that we do not see that we are in most danger, for he lay within the heart of every man. And if we continue to follow the falsehoods of what we take for granted from food, clothing, shelter, false teaching, our dumb-ing down education system, pleasures and instinct gratifications at the expense of others, then we will fall to the death of what was foretold at Fatima and what is prophesied in the Book of Revelations.

In the Gray villa at No.4 Angelikastrasse, Dresden, Germany perched on a hill overlooking the Elbe River, a young major in the Soviet secret police spent the last half of the 1980s recruiting people to spy on the West. Putin looked for East Germans who had a plausible reason to travel abroad, like professors, journalists, scientists and technicians, for whom there were acceptable cover stories. The legend was often a business trip, during which the agents could covertly link up with other spies permanently stationed in the West; according to German intelligence specialists who described Putin's task, the goal to steal Western technology or NATO secrets.

A newly revealed document shows Putin was trying to recruit agents to be trained on 'wireless communications'. But for what purpose it is not clear. Putin defends the Soviet-era intelligence service to this day. In recent comments to a writer's group in Moscow, he even seemed to excuse its role in dictator Joseph Stalin's brutal purge, saying it would be 'insincere' of him to assail the agency where he worked for so many years. Fiercely a Soviet patriot, Putin once said he could not read a book by a defector because *"I don't read books by people who have betrayed the Motherland."*

Such is the professional background of the man who won the 2000 election as Russia's new leader for a four-year term. Yet a review of his career shows that Putin previously has thrived in closed worlds, first as an intelligence agent and later in city Government. Handpicked by President Boris Yeltsin to become Prime Minister, Putin until then had never been a public figure. Putin spent 17 years as a mid-level agent in the Soviet Committee for State Security, a foreign intelligence and domestic security agency of the Soviet Union rising only to the rank of lieutenant Colonel. Later, as an aide to a prickly controversial mayor in St. Petersburg, he witnessed first the momentous finale of the Cold War. Putin saw centrally planned economies of the East stagger to disintegration. In St. Petersburg, he had a taste of the ragged path of Russia's early transition to a free market system.

He embraced the conviction that 'there is no alternative' to market democracy and soberly acknowledged Russia's economic weaknesses. He had expressed enthusiasm for asserting the role of a strong state. During his fourth term as Leader, he said the Russian economy has become 'criminalised' but initially hinted he would first tackle the powerful tycoons who lorded over the Russian economy. Putin had never campaigned for office and told an interviewer he found campaigning distasteful. "One has to be insincere and promise something which cannot be delivered," he said. "So you either have to be a fool who does not understand what you are promising or deliberately be lying."

Under his watch, we have seen several events that gave rise to concern at the time. The Cold War is long finished, but Russian intelligence has been all over the Americas ever since. Russia is accused of hacking and stealing over 1.6 million internet username and password combinations in 2015. The U.S. Security firm that holds the confidential material had gathered over 500 million email addresses and 420,000 websites that were hacked. The Kremlin is being accused of meddling in the U.S. election result and creating fake Facebook personalities, gathering 'like' followers and brainwashing them with criminal intent. In March 2018, the U.K. ex-Russian spy and his daughter were poisoned by a nerve gas reported arranged by Russia. It is difficult to know who is telling the truth. Always fact versus fiction?"

Under Putin's watch, in 2006 former Russian spy, Litvinenko died after being poisoned by a rare radioactive material in London. In 2014 a missile destroyed a Malaysia Airlines plane over the Ukraine, killing 298 people. Pro-Russian rebels were suspected of downing the airline and Ukraine's President Peter Poroshenko stated: "This is not an 'incident', it's a 'catastrophe'; this was a terrorist act." In 2015, politician Boris Nemtsov was assassinated near the Kremlin.

CHAPTER 15.

THE KREMLIN POWERHEAD

This year, 2024 marks two years since opposition activist and writer Vladimir Kara-Murza was in a coma in a Moscow hospital with an official diagnosis of acute poisoning by an unidentified substance. He received a prison sentence of 25 years, the longest for a political prisoner by the Putin regime. Russian opposition MP Ilya Ponomarev, who lives in exile in Ukraine, believes his friend has been punished for his role in the Magnitsky Act, a law of Accountability of 2012, a bipartisan bill passed by the United States Congress and signed by President Obama in December 2012. It's intent to punish Russian officials responsible for the death of Russian accountant Sergei Magnitsky in Moscow in 2009. Sadly Kara-Murza's son recently confirmed on Twitter that his father has died.

There's been a fairly extensive history of journalists, activists, and lawyers who have met messy ends in Russia, either through being shot, stabbed or having heart attacks and, in this case in particular, being poisoned. The New York Times reported, "Hackers targeted both big and small websites across the globe." Founder and chief information security officer Alex Holder said the breach was massive and was not confined to just the U.S.A. "Hackers did not target just U.S. companies, they targeted any website they could get, ranging from Fortune 500 companies to very small websites," he said. As in the rest of the Western world, the breach sparked warnings for all to step up their password security to avoid having information stolen. With the capture and jailing of international Russian Gunrunner Victor Bout and the shooting down of a Malaysia flight over Ukraine, there is tension in the air. Putin's recent major speeches show a deep resentment of what he takes to be American insistence on dominating everything. Whilst the U. S. cannot control what the Russians do, it can act to make foolish decisions on both sides less likely. When Vladimir Putin came to power in 1999, he talked ideologically but acted rationally.

Putin may have regarded the collapse of the Soviet Union as the greatest geographical disaster of the 20th Century, but he knew he couldn't re-create it. Perhaps the best metaphor is that while he brought back the Soviet national anthem, it has new words. There was no thought of returning Russia to the failed Soviet model of the planned economy and, as a self-professed believer who always wears his Baptismal cross, Putin encouraged the once-suppressed Russian Orthodox Church. Putin is a Russian patriot, but he was willing to cooperate with the West when it suited his interest.

One of the first leaders to offer condolences after the 9/11 attacks, Putin shared Russia's intelligence on Al Qaeda with the United States. However, he did not hesitate to protect Russia's interest against the West in 2008. Putin undercut any thought of NATO expansion into Georgia by launching a war against its extremely vehement pro-west president. Putin's challenges were carefully calibrated to minimise any repercussions while maximising gains. He shut off gas to Ukraine, un-leashed hackers on Estonia, and sent troops into Georgia, but he made sure the costs of his asserting regional hegemony were limited, bearable, and short-term. The annexation of Crimea, by any rational calculation, did not make sense, with Russia's already immense influence on the Peninsula, but without the need to subsidise it, as Ukraine had. The Russian Black Sea Fleet's position in the Crimean Sea port of Sevastopol was secured until 2042 and any invasion would anger the West and force support to whatever government took the place of the administration in Kyiv. Putin's actions at home in Russia are eschewing the pragmatism that marked his first administration. Instead of being an arbiter, brokering a consensus among various clans and interests, today's Putin is increasingly autocratic. His circle of allies and advisors has shrunk to those who share his exact ideas. Sober technocrats such as the Foreign Affairs minister and Defence Minister played seemingly no role in the decision to take over Crimea and were expected to execute the orders from the top.

This is one of the new themes of Russian politics: The conflation of loyalty to the Kremlin with patriotism. The dissidents at home, from journalists failing to toe the official line to protesters on the street, are castigated as 'foreign agents' from the West, whom Putin has come to see as an increasing threat to Russia's identity. As a result Putin's relationship with Russia's elite–now often foreign-educated, usually well-travelled, and always interested in economic prospects abroad-has become tortuous. Having provided members of the elite with opportunities in his first presidency, Putin not only mistrusts the Elite now but sees it as unpatriotic. Putin's view is the Elite are 'determined to steal and remove capital and do not link their future to that of their country, the place where they earn their money.' His response is a program of prompting major Russian telecom, metals and truck manufacturing to announce their return to Russia. Putin's powerful investigation committee promised a crackdown on schemes designed to transfer money out of the country. Perhaps the world should have paid more attention when Putin launched a 'Year of Culture' in 2014: 'A year of "emphasis on our cultural roots, patriotism, values and ethics."

The imperialism that has sprung up from Putin's revived emphasis on the Russian identity cannot be compared with either its Tsarist or Soviet forebears. The Tsarist Empire was driven by expansionist logic that would gladly push Russian boundaries as far as they could stretch. This was ethnic Russian, not Russian by citizenship. By contrast, Soviet imperialism embodied, theoretically a political ideology greater than any one people or culture and a rhetoric of internationalism and evangelism. Putin has spent considerable effort in forging a new Russian nationalism. Absent is the antisemitism of the Russian Empire, and the widespread racism and hostility visible in much of Russian society is not reflected in his government policy. Putin thinks 'the ethnic Russian people are, without a doubt, the backbone, the fundament, the cement of multinational Russia.' In other words, though ethnic Russians do not rule the state, they provide the foundations for the 'Russian Civilisation.'

It is a return to the time-honoured belief that there is something unique about Russia rooted not in ethnic identity but in culture and history. A belief that began when the country became the chief stronghold of Eastern Orthodoxy after the fall of Constantinople. Putin stated in 2012: ['We need to link historical eras and get an understanding that the simple truth Russia did not begin in 1917, or even in 1991, but, rather, that we have a continuous history spanning over 1000 years and we must rely on it to find inner strength and purpose in our national development.'] Putin's concept of what it means to be Russian combines the stern-jawed heroism of Soviet defenders of Stalingrad with the exuberant loyalty of the Tsar's Cossacks. Putting humanism and ascetic moralism aside, it's a version of Russian history and philosophy cherry-picked to support Putin's notion of national exceptionalism. Putin exemplifies and justifies his belief in a Russian singular place in history. The romantic necessity of obedience to the strong ruler- whether managing to endure circumstances or defending the people from cultural corruption the role of the Orthodox Church in defending the Russian soul and ideal. This is the centre of Putin's imperial vision: The pragmatic political fixer of the '2000s' now genuinely believes that Russian culture is both exceptional and threatened and that he is the man to save it.

Putin does not see himself as aggressively expanding an empire so much as defending against the 'chaotic darkness' that will ensue if he allows Russia to be politically encircled abroad and culturally colonised by Western values. The notion of empire-building based on a civilisation is crucial to understanding Putin. Neighbouring countries, such as those in the South Caucasus, he believes ought to recognise they are part of the Russian sphere of influence, in defensive perimeters and its economic hinterland. But, he stops short of wanting forcefully to bring them under direct dominion because they are not ethnic Russians.

Putin does insist, however, that Moscow is the protector of all Russians worldwide i.e. Russians, Russian speaking, Russian culture and Russian Orthodox faith. These are 'ours.' despite his mission to 'gather the Russian lands", this does not mean occupation, but helps define what he thinks is Russia's birthright. Putin is putting as much effort into defending a vision of 'Russian civilisation' at home as abroad. He has drawn connections between his past as a Patriot, an Orthodox believer, and a social conservative and between his views and State policy and has a scant interest in enforcing a social agenda.

The Russian Orthodox Church comes increasingly to the fore as a symbol and bastion of Putin's view of traditional values and all that they mean for the new imperialism. The Russian Orthodoxy was never an especially evangelical faith, concentrating on survival and purity over expansion. Much the same could be said of Putin's worldview. In Putin's previous presidency, the Church was supportive, but just one of many allies. Now though, from the pulpit to television programs, the Church is one of the most consistent and visible supporters of Putin's state-building project. The Church has long believed that 'Russian people are a divided nation on its historical territories, which has the right to be reunited in a single public body.' Speaking at the Valday International Discussion Club (2013) Putin warned against "mechanically copying other countries' experiences because the question of finding and strengthening national identity is fundamental for Russia." It is a quest he has taken upon himself in the name of personal and national greatness: "A people with a destiny cannot be allowed to let themselves, their country, and their mission down." All this helps to explain the difficulty the Western Governments have in understanding and dealing with him.

It seems that much is lost in translation between the Kremlin and the White House. Putin is not a lunatic or even a fanatic. Instead, just as there are believers who become pragmatists in office, he has made the unusual reverse journey.

Putin has come to see his role in Russia's destiny as great, unique and inextricably connected. Even if this is merely an empire of, and in, his mind, with hazy boundaries and dubious intellectual underpinnings. This is the construct with which the rest of the world will have to deal, so long as Putin remains in the Kremlin. 'I cannot imagine my own country in isolation from Europe and what we often call a civilised world' said Putin, who was still acting president after Yeltsin's sudden resignation on New Year's Eve 1999., Putin anniversary of acceding to power finds Russia has changed beyond recognition from the chaotic, open free-for-all it was under Yeltsin. Internationally it faces isolation, sanctions, and a new Cold War. At home, despite the economic decline, Putin's perhaps the highest rating of any Kremlin Leader -

with approval rating that topped 86% in 2017 and 88% in 2024. (Kremlin Statistics). Love him or hate him, it's hard to deny that Putin has made a huge impact on his country and the world.

The Ukrainian conflict has ruptured relations between Russia and the West over recent years, and is merely the latest example of Putin asserting Russia's 'rights' in its former backyard, known in Russia as 'the near abroad'. Those who were surprised by Putin's annexation of Crimea and the subsequent Russian-fuelled conflict in eastern Ukraine should re-member six years earlier he set the mould for the 'Putin doctrine' in Georgia. Russia would use troops to protect its interests in a sphere of influence increasingly hemmed in by NATO's advance. The US blinked first. In a News of the World interview in June 2017, the Russian President heralded 'common history' with the former Soviet state and said he 'hoped this period in life and history with Ukraine and the Ukrainian people will come to an end.' The charitable view of Putin's foreign policy is that he stands up to Western hegemony and, with China, acts as a balance to the military and political power of the United States.

Russia may well be the wedge that hedges any immediate threat of escalation by either North Korea or the United States of a likely nuclear war. Perhaps Putin is the key that unlocks the door of peace not war between East and West in the not-to-distant future. Always a vocal proponent of a multipolar world, Putin has shifted in recent years towards greater economic and military cooperation with Asian countries, whose economies are hungry for Russia's energy and whose governments are less judgement of its human rights record. Recently, Putin brokered two huge deals to supply China with gas, held joint naval exercises in the Mediterranean Sea and exported Russian railroad technology to North Korea. Whilst Putin has promised to keep Russia on a market path, his critics worry about his commitment to Russia's democracy. The institutions of a broad civil society are not yet developed. The rule of law has not been entrenched. These weaknesses are, in part, a legacy of the Soviet police state of Putin's early career, when the communist Party had a monopoly of power.

Referring to the Stalin era when millions went to prison camps and died, he stated [*"Of course, one must not forget the year 1937, but one must not keep alluding to this former experience, pretending that we do not need state security bodies." "All the 17 years of my work connected with the K.G.B. it would be insincere to say that I won't defend it." "If one now recollects those hard years connected with the activities of the security bodies and the damage they brought on society, one must keep in mind what sort of society it was. That Russia was then and now we are an entirely different country." "That country produced security bodies."*] He added that [*"Russia will treasure elements of civil society that we have got, our only gain over these years, then gradually we will be creating conditions under which those horrifying bodies of security will never be able to be revived."*] Putin's role in the blatantly misleading incarnation issued by the government about the Chechnya offensive has also been criticised. His talent for creating legends has been evident in his explanation of the war.

Putin told the writer's group that the military had been open with news media when the military has hidden information about casualties, combat events, attacks on civilians and its goals and methods. Felix Svetov, a writer who spent time in Stalin's prison camps as a child, was present at the writer's meeting, said Putin's comment does not correspond with reality. [*"Putin is a typical KGB type"*, he added, *"If snow is falling, they calmly tell you the sun is shining."*] With the continuous building of nuclear warheads and missile launching in North Korea, it is little wonder the world is fearing a nuclear war in this coming decade.

Russian peace not war philosophy will be a reversal of its past dark history and the consequences of it being the wedge that stalls any progress to a Nuclear disastrous world war outcome. The secret of this outcome is a total reversal of past actions in its destructive devastation for economies, not Russia in both World Wars and its espionage and deadly activities during the Cold War years. The geography of North Korea located in East Asia on the northern half of the Korean peninsula is pivotal to a dangerous war that could change the world forever or the olive branch of negotiation for an extended peace between East and West world economies. North Korea shares a border with three countries, China along the Amnok River, Russia along the Tumen River and South Korea along the Korean Demilitarised Zone. The Yellow Sea and the Korea Bay are on the west coast and the Sea of Japan (East Sea of Korea) is off the East Coast.

Russia is quietly boosting economic support for North Korea to try and stymie any United States-led push to oust Kim Jong Un as Moscow fears his fall would sap its regional clout and allow United States troops to deploy on Russia's eastern border. Russia is already angry about a build-up of United States-led NATO forces on its western borders in Europe and does not want any replication on its Asian flank.

Yet, while Russia has an interest in protecting North Korea, which started as a Soviet satellite state, it is not giving North Korea a free pass.: it backed United Nations sanctions against North Korea in its recent nuclear tests. At the same time, Russia is playing a fraught double game by quietly offering North Korea a slender lifeline to help it from United States-led efforts to isolate it economically. Russia has begun routing North Korean internet traffic giving North Korea a second connection to the outside world besides China. Bilateral trade with North Korea more than doubled in the first quarter of 2017 due mainly to higher oil product exports from Russia. At least eight North Korean ships have left Russia with fuel cargoes this year despite officially declaring they were bound for a different location. Russia, which shares its border with North Korea, has also resisted U.S.-led efforts to repatriate tens of thousands of North Korean workers whose remittances help keep the country's hard-line leadership afloat.

The Kremlin believes the North Korean leadership should get assurances and confidence that the United States is not in the regime change business. The prospect of regime change is a serious concern. China's economic ties to North Korea still dwarf Russia's and China remains a more powerful player in the unfolding nuclear crisis. However, whilst China is cutting back on trade to toughen its lines on its neighbour's Ballistic missile and nuclear program, Russia is increasing its support. Russia seems to be flatly opposed to regime change in North Korea. Russian politicians have repeatedly accused the United States of plotting so-called colour revolutions across the former Soviet Union and any talk of unseating any leader for whatever reason is politically toxic to the Kremlin.

Russia's recent joint military exercises with neighbouring Belarus gamed a scenario where Russian forces put down Western-backed attempts for a part of Belarus to break away. In 2011, Putin accused the U.S. Secretary of State Hillary Clinton of trying to stir unrest in Russia and he has made it clear that he wants the United States to leave Kim Jong Un alone. While condemning North Korea for what he called a provocative nuclear test. Putin recently told a forum in the eastern port of Vladivostok, that he understood North Korea's security concerns about the U.S. and South Korea. The Port of Vladivostok, a strategic city and headquarters to Russia's Pacific fleet is only 100km from Russia's border with North Korea. Russia would be fiercely opposed to any United States forces deployed in a reunited Korea. "The North Koreans know exactly how the situation developed in Iraq," Putin told the economic forum, saying Washington had used the false pretext that Baghdad had weapons of mass destruction to destroy the country and its leadership. "North Korea knows all that and sees the possession of Nuclear weapons and missile technology as their only form of self-defence. "Do you think they are going to give that up?'

Analysts say Russia's view is that North Korea's transformation into a Nuclear State, though incomplete, is permanent and irreversible and the best the West can hope for is for North Korea to freeze elements of its program. It's all a very difficult balancing act for Russia. On the one hand, it does not want to deviate from its partners and mainly China's position on North Korea. But on the other hand, politicians in Russia understand the current situation and the level of interaction between Russia and North Korea puts Russia in a league of its own compared to China.

So despite Russia giving lukewarm backing to tighten sanctions on North Korea, Putin wants to help its economy grow and is advocating bringing it into joint projects with other countries in the region. "We need a gradual integration of North Korea into regional cooperation," Putin said. Putin's appeal to his people and those of other supportive countries has made his image and political prowess cult-like. Coupled with that his macho spirit is in keeping with the Russian ideal: a horse-riding, bear-chested, tiger-wrestling, clean-living, straight-action man. At least that's what the image makers have done for him. But what of the man behind the scenes? Rumours of his affection for Botox and his alleged relationship with an Olympic gymnast half his age also abound. The real stories don't make the Russian press, much less the News of the World. Is this the man who will be the wedge that breaks down the barriers of East and West and makes for peace in our world?

Meanwhile, in February 2024 Biden's endorsement of the seizure of Russian gold assets held in the American banking system to fund the war in Ukraine irritated Putin. He claimed it was an illegal act. It does smack off the same act the International Bank of Settlements approved for the Bank of England to transfer gold stolen by the Nazis after the invasion of Czechoslovakia during the 1930s. However, Putin and the Kremlin have no clean sheet when it comes to asset seizure. Russian officials have promised retaliatory asset seizures if the U.S. and its allies send reserves to Ukraine. Russian state media reports that the Kremlin has identified roughly $290 billion in U.S. and allied assets in Russia.

Putin has already taken physical assets from European companies, and Russian courts seized $440 million from J.P. Morgan accounts in Russia hours after President Biden signed legislation authorising the seizure of Russian foreign exchange reserves. European officials expressed specific concern that 'Euro-clear,' which is systemically important beyond holding Russian reserves, has significant exposure to Russia that could be exploited to undermine European financial stability. Former IMF chief economist Ken Rogoff warns that "[seizure] would be just, but very difficult to do given the damage Russia can unleash."*

Most U.S. allies remain wary of seizing Russian assets directly. The U.K. has expressed support for the seizure, although Italy, Germany, and France strongly question the legality and fear economic reprisal from Russia. Germany is especially worried that asset seizure could lend credence to ongoing World War II reparations claims against it. The European Commission began evaluating legal options to seize Russian assets in November 2022, but member states cannot reach an agreement, and the Commission indicates that it is unlikely to pursue outright seizure further. European Central Bank President Christine Lagarde warned: "Moving from freezing the assets to confiscating them, to disposing of them is something that needs to be looked at very carefully." Seizure could "break the international order that you want to protect; that you would want Russia and all countries around the world to respect," she added.

Nevertheless, ultimate success is far from certain. Ukraine's ties with NATO are growing stronger. Zelenskyy's government has survived, as has Ukraine as an independent state. What little progress Russia has made on the battlefield has come at a horrific cost in men and armaments. It remains to be seen if Putin achieves his aims.

A totalitarian form of government in which the state has no limits in authority and does whatever it wants is a thing of the past. Nazi Germany and Stalinist Russia showed what the end of humanity would look like, and still terrifies us. But it's important to understand that totalitarianism didn't just spring up out of a social vacuum. As Hannah Arendt explains in The Origins of Totalitarianism, it is, rather, just one possibility along a path that most countries are on at one time or another. And that is why it is so important to understand what it is.

CHAPTER 16.

TOTALITARIAN WORLD RULERS

"Totalitarianism is a form of government that attempts to assert total control over the lives of its citizens. It is characterised by strong central rule that attempts to control and direct all aspects of individual life through coercion and repression. It does not permit individual freedom." So says the Britannica definition. So in a nutshell individual freedoms are denied by the government- with no freedom of speech, religion, education or freedom of information.

The template for totalitarian rule by a government over its people was first applied by the laws enacted by various governments in Australia as they relate to Aboriginal Australians. These laws were copied by the South African Government in the introduction of Apartheid and both in Stalin's Russia and Hitler's Germany. The same laws they applied in race discrimination to their people where they were considered inferior.

Government legislation in Australia has historically sought to control and regulate the lives of Aboriginal people. This was primarily done through a range of policies and laws that were designed to assimilate Aboriginal people into European-Australian society and exert control over their lives. Some examples of government legislation that controlled Aboriginal lives include the Protection Acts: These laws were established in the 19th and early 20th centuries and were intended to "protect" Aboriginal people by placing them under the control of government-appointed protectors. These laws severely restricted the freedom of Aboriginal people and gave the government broad powers to determine where they could live, work, and socialise. Once in place, the government of the day moved to implement its Assimilation policies: During the 20th century, the Australian government implemented assimilation policies that aimed to absorb Aboriginal people into the broader Australian population. These policies often involved removing Aboriginal children from their families and placing them in government-run institutions or with non-Indigenous families. The most well-known example of this was the government's forced removal of Aboriginal children, known as the Stolen Generations. And then came Land control laws:

The Australian government passed laws that have restricted Aboriginal people's land rights and access to traditional lands. This has had a significant impact on Aboriginal culture and traditional practices. Then came Discriminatory laws: Throughout Australia's history, there have been various discriminatory laws that have targeted Aboriginal people, such as laws that restricted their movement, employment opportunities, and access to education and healthcare. Overall, government legislation has played a significant role in controlling the lives of Aboriginal people in Australia, often resulting in significant social, cultural, and economic harm to Aboriginal communities. It is only in recent decades that there has been a concerted effort to overturn these laws and policies and work towards reconciliation and justice for Aboriginal Australians.

Old Australians have witnessed the unfair treatment of Aboriginals in their lifetime and mostly turned a blind eye to the harm our black brothers and sisters have suffered and some have died as a consequence of the extremes applied to the stolen generation and those who have been incarcerated over past decades. Similar situations existed in the locking away of native-born Africans in South Africa during Apartheid, The Gulag system of forced labour and death camps established during Joseph Stalin's reign as dictator of the Soviet Union resulted in untold millions of deaths. Likes wise in Adolf Hitler's reign of terror in one thousand forced labor concentration camps that were established by the Nazies resulting in death and extermination of millions.

One of the most disturbing things about Nazism in Germany is how quickly the country changed. They went from democracy to concentration camps in fewer than ten years. Most of us assume that the Germans of the time were different from us — *we'd* never fall for the kind of propaganda that Hitler spewed. And our democracy is too strong to be so easily dismantled. Right? Wrong.

Arendt writes that "the success of totalitarian movements ... meant the end of two illusions of democratically ruled countries...." One illusion was that most citizens were politically active and were part of a political party. However, *... the [totalitarian] movements showed that the politically neutral and indifferent masses could easily be the majority in a democratically ruled country, [and] that therefore a democracy could function according to rules which are actively recognised by only a minority. The second democratic illusion exploded by the totalitarian movements was that these politically indifferent masses did not matter, that they were truly neutral and constituted no more than the inarticulate backward setting for the political life of the nation.*

In many modern democracies, we can see evidence of indifference and pervasive feelings of helplessness. There is low voter turnout and an assumption that things will be the way they are no matter what an individual does. There is pent-up energy in apathy. Arendt suggests that the desire to be more than indifferent is what totalitarian movements initially manipulate until the individual is subsumed.

The disturbing factor in the success of totalitarianism is ... the true selflessness of its adherents: it may be understandable that a Nazi or Bolshevik will not be shaken in his conviction by crimes against people who do not belong to the movement...; but the amazing fact is that neither is he likely to waver when the monster begins to devour its children and not even if he becomes a victim of persecution himself....

How does totalitarianism incite this kind of fanaticism? How does a political organisation "succeed in extinguishing individual identity permanently and not just for the moment of collective heroic action"?

As Arendt demonstrates, both Nazi Germany and Stalinist Russia capitalised on tensions already present in society. There was essentially a massive rejection of the existing political system as ineffectual and self-serving.

The fall of protecting class walls transformed the slumbering majorities behind all parties into one great unorganised, structureless mass of furious individuals who had nothing in common except their vague apprehension that the hopes of party members were doomed, that, consequently, the most respected, articulate and representative members of the community were fools and that all the powers that be were not so much evil as they were equally stupid and fraudulent.

How does a totalitarian government harness this attitude of the masses? By completely isolating individuals through random "liquidating" (mass murder) so that "the most elementary caution demands that one avoid all intimate contacts, if possible – not to prevent discovery of one's secret thoughts, but rather to eliminate, in the almost certain case of future trouble, all persons who might have not only an ordinary cheap interest in your denunciation but an irresistible need to bring about your ruin simply because they are in danger [in] their own lives."

It's important to understand that it is simple to isolate people who already feel isolated. When you feel disconnected from the system around you and the leaders it has, when you believe that neither your vote nor your opinion matters, it's not a huge leap to feel that your very self has no importance. This feeling is what totalitarianism figured out how to manipulate through random terror that severed any form of connection with other human beings.

Totalitarianism "demands total, unrestricted, unconditional, and unalterable loyalty of the individual member. … Such loyalty can be expected only from the completely isolated human being who, without any other social ties to family, friends, comrades, or even mere acquaintances, derives his sense of having a place in the world only from his belonging to a movement."

Totalitarianism does not have an end goal in the usual political sense. Its only real goal is to perpetuate its existence. There is no one party line that, if you stick to it, will save you from persecution. Remember the random mass murders? Stalin repeatedly purged whole sections of his government just because. Fear is a requirement. The fear is what keeps the movement going.

And how do they get there? How do they get this power?

Arendt argues that there is a "possibility that gigantic lies and monstrous falsehoods can eventually be established as unquestioned facts, that man may be free to change his past at will, and that the difference between truth and falsehood may cease to be objective and become a mere matter of power and cleverness, of pressure and infinite repetition."

This battle with truth is something we see today. Opinions are being given the same weight as facts, leading to endless debates and the assumption that nothing can be known anyway.

It is this turning away from knowledge that opens the doors to totalitarianism. "Before mass leaders seize the power to fit reality to their lies, their propaganda is marked by its extreme contempt for facts as such, for in their opinion fact depends entirely on the power of the man who can fabricate it."

These fabrications form the basis of the propaganda, with different messages crafted for different audiences. Arendt makes the point that "the necessities for propaganda are always dictated by the outside world and that the movements themselves do not propagate but indoctrinate." Thus, propaganda can be understood as directed to those who are out of the control of the totalitarian movement, and it is used to convince them of its legitimacy. Then, once you are on the inside, it's about breaking down the individuality of the citizens until there is nothing but a "subdued population."

The success of the propaganda directed internally demonstrated that "the audience was ready at all times to believe the worst, no matter how absurd, and did not particularly object to being deceived because it held every statement to be a lie anyhow."

What does totalitarian rule look like? These states are not run nu cliques or gangs. There is no protected group getting rich from this control of the masses. And no one is outside the message. For example, "Stalin shot almost everybody who could claim to belong to the ruling clique and moved the members of the Politburo back and forth whenever a clique was on the point of consolidating itself."

Why no clique? One reason is that the goal of totalitarianism is not the welfare of the state. It is not economic prosperity or social advancement.

The reason why the ingenious devices of totalitarian rule, with their absolute and unsurpassed concentration of power in the hands of a single man, were never tried before is that no ordinary tyrant was ever mad enough to discard all limited and local interests — economic, national, human, military — in favour of a purely fictitious reality in some indefinite distant future.

Since independent thinkers are a threat, they are among the first to be purged. Bureaucratic functions are duplicated and layered, with people being shifted all the time.

This regular violent turnover of the whole gigantic administrative machine, while it prevents the development of competence, has many advantages: it assures the relative youth of officials and prevents stabilisation of conditions which, at least in times of peace, are fraught with danger for totalitarian rule....Any chances of discontent and questioning of the status quo are eliminated by this perpetual rise of the newly indoctrinated.

The humiliation implicit in owing a job to the unjust elimination of one's predecessor has the same demoralising effect that the elimination of the Jews had upon the German professions: it makes every jobholder a conscious accomplice in the crimes of the government....

Totalitarianism in power is about keeping itself in power. By preemptively removing large groups of people, the system neutralises all those who might question it.

Possibly the one ray of hope in these systems is that because they pay no attention to governing, they are not likely to be sustainable in the long run.

The incredibility of the horrors is closely bound up with their economic uselessness. The Nazis carried this uselessness to the point of open anti-utility when amid the war, despite the shortage of building material and rolling stock, they set up enormous, costly extermination factories and transported millions of people back and forth. In the eyes of a strictly utilitarian world, the obvious contradiction between these acts and military expediency gave the whole enterprise an air of mad unreality.

But in the meantime, what these regimes create is so devastating to humanity that it would be naive to assume that humanity will always bounce back. "They have corrupted all human solidarity. Here the night has fallen on the future. When no witnesses are left, there can be no testimony."

Even though totalitarianism doesn't produce countries with a variety of strengths and robustness to fight off significant challenges, it should not be easily dismissed. The carnage they create tears apart all social fabric. And we must not assume that they exist only in the past. Thus, from Hannah Arendt, a final word of caution: "Totalitarian solutions may well survive the fall of totalitarian regimes in the form of strong temptations which will come up whenever it seems impossible to alleviate political, social, or economic misery in a manner worthy of man."

Few Republicans regard the Trump presidency as having been either abnormal or unsuccessful. In his first term, the respected "adults" around him not only blocked some of his most dangerous impulses but also kept them hidden from the public. To this day, some of these same officials rarely speak publicly against him. Why should Republican voters have a problem with Trump if those who served him don't? Regardless of what Trump's enemies think, this is going to be a battle of two tested and legitimate presidents.

Trump, meanwhile, enjoys the usual advantage of non-incumbency, namely: the lack of any responsibility. Biden must carry the world's problems like an albatross around his neck, like any incumbent, but most incumbents can at least claim that their opponent is too inexperienced to be entrusted with these crises. Biden cannot. On Trump's watch, there was no full-scale invasion of Ukraine, no major attack on Israel, no runaway inflation, no disastrous retreat from Afghanistan. It is hard to make the case for Trump's unfitness to anyone who does not already believe it. Trump enjoys some unusual advantages for a challenger, moreover. Even Ronald Reagan did not have Fox News and the speaker of the House in his pocket. To the degree there are structural advantages in the coming general election, in short, they are on Trump's side. Trump also enjoys another advantage. The national mood months after the election is one of bipartisan disgust with the political system in general.

Rarely in American history has democracy's inherent messiness been more striking. In Weimar Germany, Hitler and other agitators benefited from the squabbling of the democratic parties, right and left, the endless fights over the budget, the logjams in the legislature, and the fragile and fractious coalitions. German voters increasingly yearned for someone to cut through it all and get something anything — done. It didn't matter who was behind the political paralysis, either, whether the intransigence came from the right or the left.

Today, Republicans might be responsible for Washington's dysfunction, and they might pay a price for it in down-ballot races. But Trump benefits from dysfunction because he is the one who offers a simple answer: him. In this election, only one candidate is running on the platform of using unprecedented power to get things done, to hell with the rules. And a growing number of Americans claim to want that, in both parties. Trump is running against the system. Biden is the living embodiment of the system. Advantage: Trump.

It is hard to fault those who have taken Trump to court. He certainly committed at least one of the crimes he is charged with; we don't need a trial to tell us he tried to overturn the 2020 election. Nor can you blame those who have hoped thereby to obstruct his path back to the Oval Office. When a marauder is crashing through your house, you throw everything you can at him — pots, pans, candlesticks — in the hope of slowing him down and tripping him up. But that doesn't mean it works.

Trump's power comes from his following, not from the institutions of the American government, and his devoted voters love him precisely because he crosses lines and ignores the old boundaries. They feel empowered now, and that in turn empowers Trump. He is a bit like King Kong testing the chains on his arms, sensing that he can break free whenever he chooses. And as the rule of law has now stated he has done just that. The outcome of the trial demonstrates the judicial system's inability to contain someone like Trump and, incidentally, to reveal its impotence as a check should he become president. Indicting Trump for trying to overthrow the government proved akin to indicting Caesar for crossing the Rubicon, and just as effective. Like Caesar, Trump wields a clout that transcends the laws and institutions of government, based on the unswerving personal loyalty of his army of followers.*

I mention all this only to answer one simple question: Can Trump win the election? The answer, unless something radical and unforeseen happens, is: Of course he can. If that weren't so, the Democratic Party would not be in a mounting panic about its prospects.

If Trump does win the election, he will immediately become the most powerful person ever to hold that office. Not only will he wield the awesome powers of the American executive — powers that, as conservatives used to complain, have grown over the decades but he will do so with the fewest constraints of any president ever before him. Think of the power of a man who gets himself elected president despite indictments, courtroom appearances and perhaps even conviction. Would he even obey a directive of the Supreme Court? Or would he instead ask how many armoured divisions the chief justice has?

Will a future Congress stop him? Presidents can accomplish a lot these days without congressional approval, as even Barack Obama showed. The one check Congress has on a rogue president, namely, impeachment and conviction, has already proved all but impossible even when Trump was out of office and wielded modest institutional power over his party.

What about the desire for reelection, a factor that constrains most presidents? Trump might not want or need a third term, but were he to decide he wanted one, as he has sometimes indicated, would the 22 Amendment block him any more effectively from being president for life than the Supreme Court, if he refused to be blocked? Why should anyone think that amendment would be more sacrosanct than any other part of the Constitution for a man like Trump, or perhaps more importantly, for his devoted supporters?

As a reminder to the reader, Trump often uses extracts from Hitler's *Mein Kampf* in his public rhetoric and seems to have a template for his rise to power along the lines of Hitler's rise. Trump may well be more dangerous to democracy this time around than his previous first term as president.

CHAPTER 17

THE PARALLELS OF HISTORY

A final constraint on presidents has been their desire for a glittering legacy, with success traditionally measured in terms that roughly equate to the well-being of the country. But is that the way Trump thinks? Yes, Trump might seek a great legacy, but it is strictly his glory that he craves. As with Napoleon, who spoke of the glory of France but whose narrow ambitions for himself and his family brought France to ruin, Trump's ambitions, though he speaks of making America great again, clearly begin and end with himself. As for his followers, he doesn't have to achieve anything to retain their support — his failure to build the wall in his first term in no way damaged his standing with millions of his loyalists. They have never asked anything of him other than that he triumphs over the forces they hate in American society. And that, we can be sure, will be Trump's primary mission as president.

Having answered the question of whether Trump can win, we can now turn to the most urgent question: Will his presidency turn into a dictatorship? The odds are, again, pretty good.

It is worth getting inside Trump's head a bit and imagining his mood following an election victory. He will have spent the previous year, and more, fighting to stay out of jail, plagued by myriad persecutors and helpless to do what he likes to do best: exact revenge. Think of the fury that will have built up inside him, a fury that, from his point of view, he has worked hard to contain. As he once said, "I think I've been toned down if you want to know the truth. I could tone it up."

Indeed he could and will. We caught a glimpse of his deep thirst for vengeance in his Veterans Day promise to "root out the Communists, Marxists, Fascists, and Radical Left Thugs that live like vermin within the confines of our Country, lie, steal, and cheat on Elections, and will do anything possible, whether legally or illegally, to destroy America, and the American Dream."

Note the equation of himself with "America and the American Dream." It is he they are trying to destroy, he believes, and as president, he will return the favour.

The Trump administration will be filled with people who will not need explicit instruction from Trump, any more than Hitler's local Gauleiters needed instruction. In such circumstances, people " work toward the Fuhrer," which is to say, they anticipate his desires and seek favour through acts they think will make him happy, thereby enhancing their influence and power in the process.

Nor will it be difficult to find things to charge opponents with. History is unfortunately filled with instances of unfairly targeted officials singled out for being on the wrong side of a particular issue at the wrong time the State Department's "China Hands" of the late 1940s, for instance, whose careers were destroyed because they happened to be in positions of influence when the Chinese Communist Revolution occurred. Today, there is the whiff of a new McCarthyism in the air. Republicans insist that Biden himself is a " communist," that his election was a " communist takeover: and that his administration is a " communist regime."

So, the Trump administration will have many avenues to persecute its enemies, real and perceived. Think of all the laws now on the books that give the federal government enormous power to surveil people for possible links to terrorism, a dangerously flexible term, not to mention all the usual opportunities to investigate people for alleged tax evasion or violation of foreign agent registration laws. The IRS under both parties has occasionally looked at depriving think tanks of their tax-exempt status because they espouse policies that align with the views of the political parties. What will happen to the think-tanker in a second Trump term who argues that the United States should ease pressure on China? Or is the government official rash enough to commit such thoughts to official papers? It didn't take more than that to ruin careers in the 1950s.

And who will stop the improper investigations and prosecutions of Trump's many enemies? Will Congress? A Republican Congress will be busy conducting its inquiries, using its powers to subpoena people, accusing them of all kinds of crimes, just as it does now. Will it matter if the charges are groundless? And of course, in some cases, they will be true, which will lend even greater validity to a wider probe of political enemies.

Will Fox News defend them, or will it instead just amplify the accusations? The American press corps will remain divided as it is today, between those organisations catering to Trump and his audience and those that do not. But in a regime where the ruler has declared the news media to be "enemies of the state," the press will find itself under significant and constant pressure. Media owners will discover that a hostile and unbridled president can make their lives unpleasant in all sorts of ways.

How will Americans respond to the first signs of a regime of political persecution? Will they rise in outrage? Don't count on it. Those who found no reason to oppose Trump in the primaries and no reason to oppose him, in general, are unlikely to experience a sudden awakening when some former Trump-adjacent official finds himself under investigation for goodness knows what. They will know only that Justice Department prosecutors, the IRS, the FBI and several congressional committees are looking into it. And who is to say that those being hounded are not tax cheaters, or Chinese spies, or perverts, or whatever they might be accused of? Will the great body of Americans even recognise these accusations as persecution and the first stage of shutting down opposition to Trump across the country?

The Trump dictatorship will not be a communist tyranny, where almost everyone feels the oppression and has their lives shaped by it. In conservative, anti-liberal tyrannies, ordinary people face all kinds of limitations on their freedoms, but it is a problem for them only to the degree that they value those freedoms, and many people do not. The fact that this tyranny will depend entirely on the whims of one man will mean that Americans' rights will be conditional rather than guaranteed. But if most Americans can go about their daily business, they might not care, just as many Russians and Hungarians do not care.

But even if the opposition were to become strong and unified, it is not obvious what it would do to protect those facing persecution. The opposition's ability to wield legitimate, peaceful and legal forms of power will already have been found wanting in this election cycle when Democrats and anti-Trump Republicans threw every legitimate weapon against Trump and still failed. Will they turn instead to illegitimate, extralegal action? What would that look like?

Americans might take to the streets. Many people will likely engage in protests against the new regime, perhaps even before it has had a chance to prove itself deserving of them. But then what? Even in his first term, Trump and his advisers on more than one occasion discussed invoking the Insurrection Act. No less a defender of American democracy than George H.W. Bush invoked the act to deal with the Los Angeles riots of 1992. It is hard to imagine Trump not invoking it should "the Communists, Marxists, Fascists, and Radical Left Thugs" take to the streets. One suspects he will relish the opportunity.

Should Trump be successful in launching a campaign of persecution and the opposition prove powerless to stop it, then the nation will have begun an irreversible descent into dictatorship. With each passing day, it will become harder and more dangerous to stop it by any means, legal or illegal. Try to imagine what it will be like running for office on an opposition ticket in such an environment. In theory, the midterm elections in 2026 might hold hope for a Democratic comeback, but won't Trump use his considerable powers, both legal and illegal, to prevent that? Trump insists and no doubt believes that the current administration corruptly used the justice system to try to prevent his reelection. Will he not consider himself justified in doing the same once he has all the power? He has, of course, already promised to do exactly that: to use the powers of his office to persecute anyone who dares challenge him.

This is the trajectory we are on now. Is descent into dictatorship inevitable? No. Nothing in history is inevitable. Unforeseen events change trajectories. Readers of this book will no doubt list all of how it is arguably too pessimistic and doesn't take sufficient account of this or that alternative possibility. Maybe, despite everything, Trump won't win. Maybe the coin flip will come up heads and we'll all be safe. And maybe even if he does win, he won't do any of the things he says he's going to do. You may be comforted by this if you choose.

What is certain, however, is that the odds of the United States falling into dictatorship have grown considerably because so many of the obstacles to it have been cleared and only a few are left. If it then seemed unimaginable that an American president would try to remain in office after losing an election, that obstacle was cleared in 2020. And if no one could believe that Trump, having tried and failed to invalidate the 2020 election and stop the counting of electoral college votes, has nevertheless reemerged as the unchallenged leader of the Republican Party in 2024 and potentially the president again of the United States. In just a few years, America has gone from being relatively secure in a democracy to being a few short steps, and a matter of months, away from the possibility of a dictatorship. It remains to be seen if elected, Trump will follow a course similar to that of Adolf Hitler, causing chaos in America, a police state, the destruction of its economy and that of the West, and bringing about the demise of Western democracy as we know it.

What we have of Hitler's speeches are mostly recorded, and they're not always particularly coherent. What you see in efforts to compile his speeches are scholars trying to piece together what they sounded like. So, it's a little bit like going to watch a standup comedian who's hitting all of his great lines. You see it again and again Hitler repeating himself. He'll repeat the same lines or the same sentiment on different occasions. With Trump, whatever else you might say about him, he knows what kinds of lines generate the kinds of reactions that he wants. The purpose of the rallies is to have applause lines because that creates good media, that creates video. And if he repeats his lines again and again, it increases the likelihood that a particular line will be repeated in media reporting.

The spectacle and social glue of mass rallies are also key. In controversial comments to Playboy magazine, the late British singer David Bowie once observed: "Adolf Hitler was one of the first rock stars. Look at some of his films and see how he moved. I think he was quite as good as Jagger. It's astounding. And boy, when he hit that stage, he worked an audience. Good God! He was no politician. He was a media artist. He used politics and theatrics and created this thing that governed and controlled the show for 12 years. The world will never see his like again."*

Well, don't bet on it. Trump's rallies are typical rollicking affairs, the atmosphere part circus, part concert, part sports, bringing like-minded people together as ritualistically as the church. In all weathers, they share a collective sense of grievance and also find ways to have fun. In small towns that often feel left behind by big cities, they can represent the biggest event of the year and offer the thrill of live performance in an otherwise digitally saturated age.

De Berg comments: "If you look at the lives of many ordinary Germans during the Weimar Republic immediately after the First World War, when the economy wasn't doing well and there were all sorts of problems, many of them could not afford to enjoy all sorts of spectacles but they could go to a Hitler rally.

You can go to a Trump rally and that creates a feeling of solidarity, a community of feeling; "You can go to a Trump rally as well and that creates a feeling of solidarity, a community of feeling, which of course is at the same time the dangerous thing because people then identify with each other. They lose their individuality, they lose their critical capacity, and at the same time all together they identify with a political leader, so the political leader can do whatever he wants."

There is also something alarmingly familiar about how the Republican party thought it could co-opt and control Trump, only to find itself capitulating and being recast in his image. One by one the party stalwarts have fallen into line, abandoning long-held principles, while dissenters have been purged. De Berg continues: "Hitler goes from 2.6% of the vote in '928, meaning more than 97% of the electorate don't want him, to the Nazi party becoming the biggest party in 1932. Then these conservative politicians say, OK, we've got this political nincompoop here but he's a populist and he's popular, the people like him. If we try and make this guy vice-chancellor then he can do our bidding.

"Hitler says no, I'm not going to be vice-chancellor, I want to be chancellor, but they still think that he is going to do what they want and push through their policies. One of these conservative politicians memorably said, 'We've hired him.' Hitler manipulated them and he became chancellor and from there on in it all goes disastrously wrong with German society." He adds: "One of the most worrying things for me about Trump is the way he has managed to transform what you thought was very rightwing but ultimately rational politicians into people who have become Trump-like.

"What happened was not that they manipulated Trump but Trump ended up manipulating them and then, in effect, just taking over the Republican party. All these people had to renounce all the things they used to believe in international free trade agreements, a forward-leaning role for America in the world."

There is, the academic warns, the method in Trump's madness: the buffoonery, chaos and word salad speeches may be more calculated than they appear. "I would like people to become more aware of how incredibly consciously Trump is going about doing what he's doing, how incredibly cunning and devious he's been. People should not underestimate this guy.

Hitler's Germany was not only the first to use or advance television, rocketry, and computers, it was the first to build a national freeway network throughout the country, address national health issues, restrict the private ownership and use of firearms, attack the abuse of alcohol and tobacco and pass laws protecting the environment and wage war against cancer. Cunningly Hitler gained the support of the wealthy elite and spoke openly in support of their conservative ideals in areas of rearmament and foreign policy. His social programs were a liberal people's dream come true. He extended anti-gun control to an already mainly unarmed population which allowed the Nazis to gain and multiply their arms and power over the people. He had once stated 'It would be foolish to allow the subject race to possess arms. History shows that all conquerors who have allowed the subject race to carry arms have prepared for their downfall. I would go so far as to say that the supply of arms to the underdogs is a sine quo non for the overthrow of any sovereignty." By March 1938 the Nazies codified in the Nazi Weapons Act, new stringent gun laws were strengthened by asserting that only Nazis could own weapons.

The Nazis inherited a list of firearms owners and their firearms gave them the lawful right of "Gun Control" and the right to seize privately held firearms from persons who were considered not reliable to the Nazi cause. Knowing who owned firearms the Nazis had only to revoke annual ownership permits or decline to renew them.

After the assassination of John F Kennedy, a cry for gun control rang across America, and the media was in high gear to promote that agenda. Then in April 1968, the murder of Martin Luther King Jr. and Robert Kennedy in June was also murdered. So the Gun Control Act of 1968 was passed in October which offered a draconian solution that settled for a compromise that still fulfils the original agenda. The new legislation stated that only licensed dealers could send and receive firearms across state lines, thus ending mail-order sales. It also allowed bureaucrats in Washington to decide what types of firearms Americans could own. The term 'sporting' gun was not clearly defined allowing a whole class of firearms to be banned.

Given the parallels between the Nazi Weapons Act of 1938 and the Gun Control Act of 1968 in America, the law sharply cuts back on the civil rights of law-abiding American citizens, when drawing upon the Nazi parallels. It seems that the right to bear arms as specified in the Second Amendment in America still stands, but it remains to be seen if a Trump dictatorship challenges this by overturning the constitution in favour of militant state control of arms like that orchestrated by Hitler's Nazies domestically in their early years in power.

Most people know Rockefeller's control over oil but are not aware of the extent of their wealth and influence in the arena of modern medicine and drugs. The medical and drug industry is controlled by Rockefeller's medical monopoly largely through directors of pharmaceutical boards representing Chase Bank, Standard Oil, and other aligned group entities. By way of example, the American College of Surgeons maintains its monopolistic control over hospitals through the powerful Hospital Survey Committee whose members each represent the Rockefeller control. Whilst these controls are represented also by big pharmaceutical and natural medicine monopolies throughout America and the Western world and can manipulate health policy through the likes of the World Health Organisation, it does take much of a shift from democratic policies to a dictatorship to see how this can all change.*

To cite an example during the Third Reich, a politically extreme, antisemitic variation of eugenics determined the course of state policy. Hitler's regime touted the "Nordic race" as its eugenic ideal and attempted to mould Germany into a cohesive national community that excluded anyone deemed hereditarily "less valuable" or "racially foreign." Public health measures to control reproduction and marriage aimed at strengthening the "national body" by eliminating biologically threatening genes from the population. Many German physicians and scientists who had supported racial hygiene ideas before 1933 embraced the new regime's emphasis on biology and heredity, the new career opportunities, and the additional funding for research.

Hitler's dictatorship, backed by sweeping police powers, silenced critics of Nazi eugenics and supporters of individual rights. After all educational and cultural institutions and the media came under Nazi control, racial eugenics permeated German society and institutions. Jews, considered "alien," were purged from universities, scientific research institutes, hospitals, and public health care. Persons in high positions who were viewed as politically "unreliable" met a similar fate. Echoing ongoing eugenic fears, the Nazis trumpeted population experts' warnings of "national death" and aimed to reverse the trend of falling birthrates. The Marital Health Law of October 1935 banned unions between the "hereditarily healthy" and persons deemed genetically unfit. Getting married and having children became a national duty for the "racially fit." In a speech on September 8, 1934, Hitler proclaimed: "In my state, the mother is the most important citizen." Eugenicists had expressed concerns about the effects of alcohol, tobacco, and syphilis. The Nazi regime sponsored research undertook public education campaigns, and enacted laws that together aimed at eliminating "genetic poisons" linked to birth defects and genetic damage to later generations.

CHAPTER 18.

RULES OF CHURCH AND STATE

On July 14, 1933, the Nazi dictatorship fulfilled the long-held dreams of eugenics proponents by enacting the Law for the Prevention of Offspring with Hereditary Diseases ("Hereditary Health Law"), based on a voluntary sterilisation law drafted by Prussian health officials in 1932. Individuals who were subject to the law were those from any of nine conditions assumed to be hereditary: feeblemindedness, schizophrenia, manic-depressive disorder, genetic epilepsy, Huntington's chorea (a fatal form of dementia), genetic blindness, genetic deafness, severe physical deformity, and chronic alcoholism.

In 1936 the Reich Central Office for Combating Homosexuality and Abortion was established to step up efforts to prevent acts that obstructed reproduction. In a 1937 speech linking homosexuality to a falling birthrate, German police chief Heinrich Himmler stated: "A people of good race which has too few children has a one-way ticket to the grave."

Special hereditary health courts lent an aura of due process to the sterilisation measure, but the decision to sterilise was generally routine. Nearly all better-known geneticists, psychiatrists, and anthropologists sat on such courts at one time or another, mandating the sterilisations of an estimated 400,000 Germans. Vasectomy was the usual sterilisation method for men, and for women, tubal ligation was an invasive procedure that resulted in the deaths of hundreds of women.

In the United States, some newspaper editors noted the mass scale of the policy and feared that "Hitlerites" would apply the law to Jews and political opponents. In contrast, American eugenicists viewed the law as the logical development of earlier thinking by Germany's "best specialists" and not as "the hasty improvisation of the Hitler regime."*

The sterilisation of ethnic minorities defined as "racially foreign" was not mandated under the 1933 law. Instead, the " Blood Protection Law," announced in Nuremberg on September 15, 1935, criminalised marriage or sexual relations between Jews and non-Jewish Germans. Soon after, Nazi leaders took biological segregation a step further, privately discussing the "complete emigration" of all Jews as a goal. After the incorporation of Austria in March 1938 (the Anschluss), SS officer Adolf Eichmann coordinated the forced emigration of tens of thousands of Austrian Jews. The Nazi attacks on German and Austrian Jews and Jewish property of November 9–10, 1938—Kristallnacht—convinced many Jews remaining in the Reich that leaving was their only option for survival.*

In a Trump-controlled dictatorship, we may hear the echoes of National Socialism like the Third Reich. Facilitation with the occult, organic food practices, herbal medicines, healing plans and back-to-nature policies with an idealisation of rural life. Hitler advanced a vegetarian lifestyle. "One may agree that living is a period where it is impossible to form an idea or shape the world to come without the approval of the state that will be considered the norm, be it the palace you live in, the food you eat or the medicines you take." This may well be the future of many who may voluntarily participate in such a lifestyle promoted by a Trump dictatorship as it was by Hitler.

It was President George W Bush, the most recent of Presidents, who used religious factions to gain support for his policies and objectives. The most recent use of a religious view in the current US race to the White House is Donald Trump who has openly supported Christian churches and their congregations on his 'anti-abortion' stance. This is contra to the Biden government's pro-abortion approach to the abortion laws under constant debate in federal politics. Nothing much has been said on this subject since Harris' was appointed to run for the White House but it should not be overlooked in the vote count coming election.

In Russia Putin has always advocated the unity between church and state and has openly shown the unification of both in his leadership. However, time will tell if it is just a front to give the impression that he is' holier than thou' in his dictatorial leadership whilst doing exactly the opposite in reality.

This new wave approach may well apply to Donald Trump's role should he gain a second term in government. The parallels are there with Adolf Hitler in his use of the church in his National Socialist rule during his party's murderous reign of terror. It must not be forgotten that National Socialism was a religion- with its depth of ideology, the liturgy, and the element of hope, all helped to give the movement the character of a new faith. Goebbels consciously used religious terminologies in many of his speeches. Nazism had a total world view which naturally excluded all others. It followed that Christianity in time proved to be a rival not a friend of the Reich. Hitler hastened slowly in this regard for he needed the support of the majority of Christian churches. It may well be concluded that the Nazi future would gain support from the Evangelical Churches had the war been won. It was after all the churches that smuggled many of the Nazies out of Germany giving them a new identity in the post-war world.

One may be reminded of Hitler's conclusions in *Mein Kampf* on organised religions: " The great masses of people do not consist of philosophers, and it is just for them that faith is frequently the sole basis of a moral view of life." He also saw his fundamentalism as a reflection of National Socialism. " The greatest of Christianity was not rooted in its attempted negotiations of compromise with perhaps similarly constructed philosophical opinions of the old world." he wrote, " but in the inexorably fanatical preaching and representation of its doctrine ."

We should not forget that Hitler, despite his support early in his reign by religion, was deeply entrenched in occultism, which he privately expressed in his discourse. He saw it as a new wave of religious symbolism in the course of his views on Christianity.

The evidence that Hitler was a staunch Christian is overwhelming. He banned secular education in Germany on the basis that Christian religious instruction is essential to moral development, repeatedly vilified atheism, and although he often clashed with Catholic bishops over his ill-treatment of Jews, Hitler did not perceive himself as being anti-Christian, but rather as bringing the Church back to what he saw as its proper, traditional role in persecuting the pestilent. While negotiating the *Reichskonkordat*, Hitler said to Bishop Berning that suppressing Jews was, "doing Christianity a great service by pushing them out of schools and public functions."

There are numerous other examples, from *Mein Kampf* ("only fools and criminals would think of abolishing existing religion"), to Hitler's letters (1941: "I am now as before a Catholic and will always remain so"), to the *Gott Mit Uns* motto on German army uniforms during the Nazi era, to the Lutheran Church in Berlin, full of carvings celebrating Hitler's rise to power (including an exquisitely carved SA paramilitary trooper on the baptismal font), to the amended 1934 loyalty oath of the German military ("I swear by almighty God this sacred oath: I will render unconditional obedience to the Führer of the German Reich and people, Adolf Hitler, Supreme Commander of the Wehrmacht…").

After the Enabling Act of 1933 delivered dictatorial powers to Hitler, one of his first actions was to outlaw atheist and free-thinking groups. His public speech, after the fact, boasted that, "we have therefore undertaken the fight against the atheistic movement, and that not merely with a few theoretical declarations: we have stamped it out." In short, there is overwhelming evidence that Hitler saw himself as a Christian doing God's work (even if his church often opposed him) and that he saw atheism as one of many insults to the German nation requiring ruthless suppression.

It is the view of many that Donald Trump has deceived himself into believing that he will unite America after he breaks down every value of a democratic society, just as Adolf Hitler did in his blood lust to purify everything for God Almighty under Nazi rule,

After Adolf Hitler acceded to power in 1933, the Nazies set out to reconstruct German society. To do that, the totalitarian government attempted to exert complete control over the populace. Every institution was infused with National Socialist ideology and infiltrated by Nazi personnel in chief positions. Schools were no exception. Even before coming to power, Hitler in *Mein Kampf* had hinted at his plans for broad educational exploitation. The Ministry of Public Enlightenment and Propaganda exercised control over virtually every form of expression—radio, theatre, cinema, the fine arts, the press, churches, and schools. The control of the schools began in March 1933 with the issuing of the first educational decree, which held that "German culture must be treated thoroughly."

The Nazi government attempted to control the minds of the young and thus, among other means, intruded Nazi beliefs into the school curriculum. A major part of biology became "race science," and health education and physical training did not escape the racial stress. Geography became the study of the fatherland being fundamental. Physical training was made compulsory for all, as was youth labour service. However, much of the fundamental curriculum was not disturbed. It was more the shaping of the future in Hitler's indoctrination that took resent over all other studies: "These boys and girls enter our organisations at ten years of age, and often for the first time get a little fresh air; after four years of the Young Folk they go on to the Hitler Youth, where we have them for another four years . . . And even if they are still not complete National Socialists, they go to Labor Service and are smoothed out there for another six, seven months… And whatever class consciousness or social status might still be left . . . the Wehrmacht [German armed forces] will take care of that."

—Adolf Hitler (1938)

One major difference between the Third Reich and the Fourth in America is the lack of emphasis on the flag ceremonies and the repetitious Pledge of Allegiance. In Nazi Germany, a school day did not pass without these ceremonies. In a multicultural globalised America today, school children still recite the Pledge of Allegiance and raise the flag, but all formal ceremonies are almost none existent. In schools and adult ceremonies hardly anyone observes proper flag-raising protocols. If the Pledge of Allegiance is used in schools it is generally over a loud speaker. A student doesn't need to recite the pledge. The patriotism to One's nation is not conducive to a globalised world. The corporate logo slogans and social media presence have long since replaced what was once taken for granted. This is why I believe Donald Trump has captured the essence of propaganda in re-introducing the American flag as a symbol, of unity, as well as Adolf Hitler did with his Nazi symbol in flag-waving ceremonies.

Corporate America has captured the education system with the rising intrusion of advertising in schools. The line is blurred between education and the promotional messages portrayed to children by corporate America in online lecturers, resulting in distorted learning patterns. It is only a matter of time before bulletin boards, school, community message centres and the curriculum itself is moulded into corporate American imagery. In an ideal world funding school programs and buying equipment should be the job of parents with government subsidy, but America is not Utopia so both public and private colleges accept money from capitalists corporations and wealthy individuals who have agendas other than the formal education of children.

In the classroom and the Hitler Youth, instruction aimed to produce race-conscious, obedient, self-sacrificing Germans who would be willing to die for Führer and Fatherland. Devotion to Adolf Hitler was a key component of Hitler Youth training. German young people celebrated his birthday (April 20)—a national holiday—for membership inductions. German adolescents swore allegiance to Hitler and pledged to serve the nation and its leader as future soldiers. Schools played an important role in spreading Nazi ideas to German youth. While censors removed some books from the classroom, German educators introduced new textbooks that taught students love for Hitler, obedience to state authority, militarism, racism, and antisemitism.

From their first days in school under nazi rule, German children were imbued with the cult of Adolf Hitler. His portrait was a standard fixture in classrooms. Textbooks frequently described the thrill of a child seeing the German leader for the first time.

It has been historic for governments to exploit the young in favour of their agenda, The Nazies in the 1930s fully realised that if the younger generation could be brought to their worldview, the future of National Socialism would be assured. A prime example of modern American conflict between old and young began in the 1950s with rock n' roll music and grew full-blown with the Vietnam War. The patriotism of the anti-war movement embraced by youth was tempered by the propaganda of World War 11 and supporters of the old generation of Lyndon Johnson and Richard Nixon's stance on Vietnam. There is in this a worthy reflection of Nazi Germany where Hitler's promises of a more prosperous future held considerable sway with the younger generation, whilst the older generation mindful of The First World War and difficulties that followed were more sceptical but a complaint to the Nazies rule. Hitler's propaganda machine took control over popular culture with music, film and rallies which was another use of the divide-and-rule methodology of Nazism which had been used as far back as Fabius in Roman times.

Germans who were against National Socialism under Hitler learnt to comply in the hope that Germany would ultimately lose the war and the allies, and in particular, America, would come to their aid and ensure a better future in a free post-war world.

In today's world advancing towards a totalitarian state, and the advance of a fascist agenda in America in particular, one wonders who will come to the rescue if things go pear shape?

Whilst Nazi-occupied Europe looked hopefully towards the allied nations for liberation, if America became the first world empire to be a new Reich and fell under fascist domination, where can America look for deliverance, and for that matter the rest of the democratic countries of the world?

CHAPTER 19.

UNITED WE STAND.

Under Nazi Germany, the labour force was praised and glamorised, but the power of the unions was all but abolished as all labour matters were combined under the German Labor Front, a rigid Nazi organisation created by Hitler to replace the old labour union system. It was a typical globalist's agenda to curtail any meaningful power within the working class despite early support due to Nazi slogans and propaganda the workers soon realised it was a myth, and labour problems continued to plague the Nazi government right through to the end of the war. In light of such difficulties in Germany, the globalists in America declined to create a labour-controlling mechanism with modern America, Instead, they set out to create a successful program of buying corrupt labour leaders, making deals with crime syndicates that controlled key unions and crippled labour through federal legislation push through congress with corporate money.

The National Labor Relations Act of 1935 (NLRA). The NLRA was a major turning point in American labour history because it was supposed to put the power of government behind the right of workers to organise unions and bargain collectively with their employers about wages, hours, and working conditions. Workers originally wanted unions primarily for defensive purposes -- to protect against what they see as arbitrary decisions, such as sudden wage cuts, lay-offs, or firings. They also want a way to force management to change what they see as dangerous working conditions or overly long hours. More generally, they want more certainty, which eventually means a contract that lasts for a specified period. In the United States, as we will see, the early trade unionists also wanted the same kind of rights at work that they already had as independent citizens. And if unions grow strong, then, well, they try to go on the offensive, by asking for higher wages.

Business owners, on the other hand, don't like unions for a variety of reasons. If they are going to compete successfully in an economy that can go boom or bust, then they need a great deal of flexibility in cutting wages, hiring and firing, and adding extra hours work or trimming back work hours when need be. Wages and salaries are a very big part of their overall costs, maybe as much as 80% in many industries in the past, and still above 50% in most industries today, although there is variation. And even when business is good, small wage cuts, or holding the line on wages, can lead to higher profits. More generally, business owners are used to being in charge, and they don't want to be hassled by people they have come to think of as mere employees, not as breadwinners for their families or citizens of the same city and country.

Thus, the nature of the economic system means that there is going to be at least some degree of conflict over a wide range of issues between owners/managers and employees/workers. These conflicts are therefore best described as *class conflicts* because the two sides have many conflicting objectives even though they have to cooperate to keep the company going. The conflicts that these disagreements generate can manifest themselves in many different ways in a step-by-step escalation: workplace protests, strikes, industry-wide boycotts, massive demonstrations in cities, pressure on Congress, and voting preferences.

The prime example of 20th-century corruption and union control was with the Teamsters Union of the 1950s and early 1960s. Seattle had a starring role in the corruption scandal that engulfed the Teamsters union in the late 1950s. That's when it became clear that Dave Beck, the Seattle-based Teamster president, was stealing money from the organisation. Notorious labour leader Jimmy Hoffa, known for his close ties to mobsters, rose to power after Beck, even after coming under federal scrutiny himself. Robert F. Kennedy, chief counsel for a Senate investigating committee, led the charge to bring him to justice.

At the time, Democrats were pro-labour, but there was also labour racketeering and corruption in pockets of different unions, reporters had been digging into this, and one of them, Clark Mollenhoff, a very aggressive reporter from Iowa, convinced Kennedy to take on labour rackets. Kennedy didn't want to do it, his father did not want him to do it because he thought going after labour would hurt his brother John F. Kennedy's chances in the 1960 election, but Bobby Kennedy wanted something of his own, to achieve some sort of social good, and he was intrigued by the problem and he wanted to dig into it.*

Bobby Kennedy was very naïve about how labour unions worked, why someone would join them, and what it was like to be working class, so it was a journey of discovery for him. And Hoffa, who came up in Detroit in the bloody 1930s, just thought Kennedy was a punk, didn't understand how things worked in the real world, and so they had great personal animosity because there was a clash of class as well as good versus bad. Hoffa truly believed in labour because it meant getting the highest dollar for your labour. He very sneeringly dismissed labor leaders like Walter Reuther who saw it as part of a broader movement for social justice and fairness. Hoffa was a Republican. Everybody had his price, whether it was the businessman on the other side of the table in bargaining, the cop on the picket line or the judge who was hearing a case against a teamster. Everybody had a price, he said. What's yours?*

Beck was, as Bobby Kennedy called him, a thief. So, for example, he got the Teamsters to purchase his home up on the shores of Lake Washington. He was a wealthy man, and he was very powerful. Eisenhower made him his labour ambassador, and at the time the Teamsters were becoming the toughest, most powerful labour union in the United States. Bobby Kennedy couldn't pin down Hoffa when he dragged him before the Senate Rackets Committee hearings in 1957, 1958 and 1959, and Hoffa, who was a master of intimidation, would humiliate him public -ally so that got under Kennedy's craw. In addition, the Senate Rackets Committee hearings took down Dave Beck relatively easily. Kennedy felt guilty when he realised he knocked out Beck and then Hoffa climbed over Beck's back and became president [of the Teamsters]. Kennedy thought he could take down Hoffa relatively easily as well but he couldn't.*

Hoffa hated the Kennedys, so when he heard that Kennedy was assassinated, out of his self-interest, he was excited. As he said when asked by reporters for his reaction, `Bobby Kennedy is just another lawyer now.' In early 1964, Kennedy's Justice Department had brought two cases against Hoffa, one in Tennessee and one in Chicago, and the result was convictions in both of those. So finally after all these indictments and all these acquittals and hung juries, Hoffa got his comeuppance. The use of the Teamsters retirement fund by union members in the Mob, the part that Robert Kennedy played in attempting to break the union and make powerful people answerable to the law saw his demise by assassination like his brother JFK and Hoffa mysteriously disappear, believed to be buried somewhere in the Nevada desert killed by the bullet of a hired underworld assassin.

Hiring agencies specialising in anti-union practices have been an option available to employers from the bloody strikes of the last quarter of the nineteenth century, until today. For approximately 150 years, union organising efforts and strikes have been periodically opposed by police, security forces, national; guard units, special police forces and/or use of the United States Army. *

The Corporations Auxiliary Company, a union buster during the first half of the 20th century, would tell employers: "Our man will come to your factory and get acquainted... If he finds little disposition to organise, he will not encourage the organisation but will engineer things to keep the organisation out. If, however, there seems a disposition to organise he will become the leading spirit and pick out just the right men to join. Once the union is in the field its members can keep it from growing if they know how, and our man knows how. Meetings can be set far apart. A contract can at once be entered into with the employer, covering a long period, and made very easy in its terms. However, these tactics may not be good, and the union spirit may be so strong that a big organisation cannot be prevented. In this case, our man turns extremely radical. He asks for unreasonable things and keeps the union embroiled in trouble. If a strike comes, he will be the loudest man in the bunch and will counsel violence and get somebody in trouble. The result will be that the union will be broken up.*

In 1956, the Retail Clerks Union employed tactics that Walter Tudor, the Sears vice-president for personnel, described as "inexcusable, unnecessary and disgraceful". At a Marion, Ohio, Whirlpool plant, an LRA operative created a card file system that tracked employees' feelings about unions. Many of those he regarded as pro-union were fired. A similar practice took place at the Morton Frozen Foods plant in Webster City, Iowa. An employee recruited by LRA operatives wrote down a list of employees thought to favour a union. Management fired those workers. The list-making employee received a substantial pay increase. When the United Packinghouse Workers of America union was defeated, Nathan Shefferman, the 1950s most famous union buster, arranged a sweetheart contract with a union that Morton Frozen Foods controlled, with no participation from the workers. From 1949 through 1956, LRA earned nearly $2.5 million providing such anti-union services.

In 1957, the McClellan Committee investigated unions for corruption, and employers and agencies for union-busting activities. Labour Relations Associates was found to have committed violations of the National Labor Relations Act of 1935, including manipulating union elections through bribery and coercion, threatening to revoke workers' benefits if they organised, installing union officers who were sympathetic to management, rewarding employees who worked against the union, and spying on and harassing workers. The McClellan Committee believed that "the National Labor Relations Board [was] impotent to deal with Shefferman's type of activity."

There is little evidence that employers availed themselves of anti-union services during the 1960s or the early 1970s. However, under a new reading of the Landrum-Griffin Act, the U.S. Department of Labor took action against consulting agencies related to the filing of required reports in only three cases after 1966, and between 1968 and 1974 it filed no actions at all. By the late 1970s, consulting agencies had stopped filing reports.*

The 1970s and 1980s were an altogether more hostile political and economic climate for organised labour. Meanwhile, a new multi-billion dollar union buster industry, using industrial psychologists, lawyers, and strike management experts, proved skilled at sidestepping requirements of both the NLRA and Landrum-Griffin in the war against labour unions.] In the 1970s the number of consultants, and the scope and sophistication of their activities, increased substantially. As the number of consultants increased, the number of unions suffering National Labor Relations Board (NLRB) setbacks also increased. Labour's percentage of election wins slipped from 57 per cent to 46 per cent. The number of union decertifications tripled, with a 73 per cent loss rate for unions.*

Labour relations consulting firms began providing seminars on union avoidance strategies in the 1970s. Agencies moved from subverting unions to screening out union sympathisers during hiring, indoctrinating workforces, and propagandising against unions.*

In August 1981, the Professional Air Traffic Controllers Organisation went on strike seeking better pay and working conditions, among other issues. When the striking workers refused to obey a court order to return to work, President Ronald Reagan ordered the Federal Aviation Administration Federal fire all 11,345 strikers and hire strikebreakers to replace them. By the mid-1980s, Congress had investigated but failed to regulate, abuses by labour relations consulting firms. Meanwhile, while some anti-union employers continued to rely upon the tactics of persuasion and manipulation, other besieged firms launched blatantly aggressive anti-union campaigns. At the dawn of the 21st Century, methods of union busting have recalled similar tactics from the dawn of the 20th Century. The political environment has included the NLRB and the Department of Labor failing to enforce the labour law against companies that repeatedly violate it.*

From 1960 to 2000 the percentage of workers in the United States belonging to a labor union fell from 30% to 13%, almost all of that decline being in the private sector. This is despite an increase in workers expressing an interest in belonging to unions since the early 1980s. (In 2005, more than half of unionised private-sector workers said they wanted a union in their workplace, up from around 30% in 1984. A change in the political climate in Washington DC starting in the late 1970s "sidelined" the NLRA. Much more aggressive and effective business lobbying meant "few real limits on ... vigorous anti-union activities. ... Reported violations of the NLRA skyrocketed in the late 1970s and early 1980s. Meanwhile, strike rates plummeted, and many of the strikes that did occur were acts of desperation rather than indicators of union muscle."

Common legal tactics used by employers to prevent unionisation include forcing employees to attend anti-union meetings, known as captive audience meetings, where pro-union workers are unable to present alternative views; covering the workplace with anti-union posters, banners, or videos; instructing managers to tell workers that they may lose their jobs if they vote to unionise; and having managers hold one-on-one meetings with workers to argue it would be bad for them to vote for a union.[60] Employers' messages frequently focus on themes such as the idea that unions will drive employers out of business, that unions only care about extracting dues payments from workers, and that unionisation is unnecessary or futile.[60] Overall, US employers spend around $340 million per year on union-avoidance consultants to help them prevent employees from forming unions.

Several US corporations have also produced anti-union training materials that have been disseminated to managers or other employees.

In 2018, Amazon distributed a 45-minute union-busting training video to managers at Whole Foods, which it had acquired in 2017, instructing managers to look for warning signs that might indicate "vulnerability to organising," including the use of the term "living wage" and workers showing an "unusual interest in policies, benefits, employee lists, or other company information," and to immediately escalate potential signs of organising to general managers.

In January 2022, Target emailed store managers at the company new training documents, instructing managers to look for warning signs of union organising within their stores, including conversations among workers regarding pay, benefits, job security, or other grievances, and to coordinate with human resources to prevent unionisation.

In the early 21st century, employees at several prominent US corporations have accused their employers of engaging in illegal union-busting activities. A 2019 report from the Economic Policy Institute found that employers were charged with illegally firing workers in 19.9% of union elections, and with illegally coercing, threatening, or retaliating against workers for supporting a union in 29.6% of union elections. Overall, unfair labour practice charges were filed against employers in 41.5% of NLRB-supervised union elections that took place in 2016 and 2017, and in elections involving more than 60 voters 54.4% of employers were charged with at least one illegal act

In July 2015, theInternational Association of Machinists and Aerospace Workers union filed a complaint with the NLRB against Amazon, alleging that the company engaged in unfair labour practices by surveilling, threatening, and "informing employees that it would be futile to vote for union representation" during a union drive in 2014 and 2015 at an Amazon warehouse in Chester, Virginia.

In May 2024, workers at an Amazon warehouse in St.Peters, Missouri filed an unfair labour practice charge against the company with the NLRB, accusing the company of using "intrusive algorithms" as part of a surveillance program to deter union organising at the warehouse.[66] In June 2024, a group of 104 delivery drivers at Amazon's DIL7 facility in Skokie, Illinois, employed by contractor Four Star Express Delivery as part of Amazon's Delivery Service Partner subcontractor program, and organised with the Teamsters Local 704 union, filed unfair labour practice charges with the NLRB against both Amazon and Four Star Express as a single or joint employer, alleging that their employer terminated employees for organising a union, surveilled workers attempting to organise, implemented a hiring freeze in response to unionisation efforts, suppressed pro-union speech on employee message boards, altered terms of employment in response to union activity, and sought to permanently close the DIL7 facility in response to union organising ability.

Over the past few months, the United States has seemingly entered a new era for American unions. After decades of decline, major American unions including the Teamsters, the United Automobile Workers, the Writers Guild of America, and the Screen Actors Guild — have taken militant stances in contract negotiations. Thus far, two have chalked up considerable victories. Then we saw in October 2023 workers at Kaiser Permanente walked off the job in the largest strike of healthcare workers in U.S. history.

It seems that the public's sympathies are with workers. Unions are enjoying higher support among the public than they have in decades. That gives confidence to workers considering going out on strike. Also, I believe that unions are considering the leverage that the tight labour market gives them. They are highly motivated to negotiate advantageous contracts now, so they can lock in their enhanced power. Finally, many of the unions that have been engaged in these high-profile labour actions are in sectors where big, transformational change is either just on the horizon or already here. For example, the Hollywood strikes have focused on what the impact of AI is going to be in their work and the UAW strike is in part about how the auto industry is going to transition to an EV future. Workers want to have a voice in how these transformations impact them – active unions give them a meaningful seat at the table as decisions are made that will define the future. So in in the past three years, we have seen union activity on the rise in numerous actions for workers' rights:

Looking back on the power of the worker in Germany, .before 1933 the Nazis had lacked support amongst the workers who tended to vote for the communists of the early years.1933, Hitler and the fascist Nazi party took power. At the time, the German free trade union movement was one of the largest in the world. When Hitler was appointed Chancellor on Jan. 30, 1933, he did not have a majority in the German parliament (Reichstag). To consolidate power, in February 1933, the Nazi Party set fire to the Reichstag and then blamed it on a "communist plot" to overthrow the government. The fire was used to promote the "Reichstag Fire Decree," which suspended all civil liberties and democratic rights, including habeas corpus, the privacy of the mail and telephone, freedom of expression and the press, the right to public assembly, and protections against search and seizure in relations to homes and property. Opposition leaders were arrested. All these draconian measures were used to allow Hitler to rule by decree. (Shades of Jan 6 Trump's attempted take over of Congress?)

However, the German labour movement's seven million union members still posed a real threat to the Nazis' fascist consolidation of power, despite the unions' weakened state. The Nazi Party's paramilitary "stormtroopers" (fascist armed thugs) stepped up attacks on union members and their offices in dozens of towns. The day after 1933's May Day International Workers' Day celebrations, real and free labour unions were outlawed throughout the country.

Police and "stormtroopers" raided labour union offices across the country. Union funds were confiscated, and these organisations dissolved. The Nazis beat union officials, murdered many, and arrested many more. Leaders were imprisoned in concentration camps, including Dachau, which was specially built to imprison and murder trade unionists, members of the Communist Party (KPD), the Social Democratic Party (SPD) and other dissidents. The need for German rearmament made it important that workers were productive and controlled. The Nazis set up three organisations that would manage German workers. The Labour Front was a Nazi organisation that replaced trade unions, which were banned. It set wages and nearly always followed the wishes of employers, rather than employees. Secondly was the KdF-strength through joy scheme which gave workers rewards for effort-evening classes, theatre trips, picnics, and even very cheap or free holidays. The purpose of the KdF was to support the Führer thank him and keep everyone happy after abolishing the trade unions.

Dr Robert Ley was in charge of the KdF, and one of its popular schemes was the Volkswagen - the people's car. It was possible to pay for the car in instalments, and the buyer would only receive the car after they had paid the balance in full. When World War Two started in 1939, the car factories had to turn their attention to manufacturing arms. As a result, many Germans lost their money, and there were demonstrations against Ley.

Thirdly, there was beauty through labour. The job of this organisation was to help Germans see that work was good, and that everyone who could work should. It also encouraged factory owners to improve conditions for workers. The Beauty of Labour organisation improved conditions in some workplaces with improved canteens, toilets and sometimes even sports facilities.

Apart from forced labour in the concentration camps, it appears that logistically railway, shipping, car industries and war machine manufacturers were not controlled as rigidly by the Nazies as others in their jobs, despite loss of wages and having to curtail Nazies' work rules. Hitler had difficulty applying Nazi policies to the former union workers during the war years and preferred to focus his attention more on building the Auto-barn and clockwork railway networks in preference to controlling the logistics workforce.

There are many parallels to the Nazi era and modern America. The attacks of 9/11 and the Reichstag fire, Bush's Patriot Act and Hitler's Enabling Act, the use of German army reserves to attack Poland, and Bush's use of reserves in attacking Afghanistan and Iraq to avoid a military draft are actions in common.

Today it's not just the politicians that must be careful of voicing their opinion in the new American empire. We see Nazi-like demonstrators being herded up and routinely fenced in for speaking their minds in the workplace or arrested for public demonstrations. The internet, AI and surveillance technology make it difficult for public discourse without offending some officials or others.

Donald Trump's campaign for a second term as President is not to be misunderstood. His drive to fly the 'Star Spangled' banner at every rallying point of his followers under the slogan " Make America Great Again" is disguising the truth of his lust for power and control of everything that is American. His first term as President is a reference point for bringing down American values and the Constitution with the ultimate aim of his dictatorship. Like the Nazi Third Reich, the tool of propaganda is at the forefront of his tools of public control.

CHAPTER 20.

THE PROPAGANDA MACHINE

To explore the dangers that await America we have only to revisit Nazi Germany under Hitler and the amazing propaganda machine that was created and affected the German people when Goebbels was appointed Minister for Propaganda.

Interestingly it was Sigmund Freud's nephew Edward Bernays who tapped into the idea of propaganda upon reading some of Uncle Sigmund's work on the conscious mind and means of manipulation. While no single person can claim exclusive credit for the ascendancy of advertising in American life, no one deserves credit more than a man most of us have never heard of: Edward Bernays. Often referred to as "the father of public relations," Bernays in 1928 published his seminal work, Propaganda, in which he argued that public relations is not a gimmick but a necessity: he argued not to fight misfortune but be a part of the solution:

The conscious and intelligent manipulation of the organised habits and opinions of the masses is an important element in a democratic society. Those who manipulate this unseen mechanism of society constitute an invisible government which is the true ruling power of our country. We are governed, our minds are moulded, our tastes formed, and our ideas suggested, largely by men we have never heard of.... It is they who pull the wires that control the public mind.

The year after his birth, the Bernays family moved to New York, and Edward Bernays later graduated from Cornell with a degree in agriculture. But instead of farming, he chose a career in journalism, eventually helping the Woodrow Wilson Administration promote the idea that US efforts in World War I were intended to bring democracy to Europe.

Having seen how effective propaganda could be during war, Edward Bernays wondered whether it might prove equally useful during peacetime.

Yet propaganda had acquired a somewhat pejorative connotation (which would be further magnified during World War II), so Bernays promoted the term "public relations." Drawing on the insights of his Uncle Sigmund – a relationship Bernays was always quick to mention – he developed an approach he dubbed "the engineering of consent." He provided leaders with the means to "control and regiment the masses according to our will without their knowing about it." To do so, it was necessary to appeal not to the rational part of the mind, but the unconscious.

Bernays acquired an impressive list of clients, ranging from manufacturers such as General Electric, Procter & Gamble, and the American Tobacco Company, to media outlets like CBS and even politicians such as Calvin Coolidge. To counteract President Coolidge's stiff image, Bernays organised "pancake breakfasts" and White House concerts with Al Jolson and other Broadway performers. and with Bernay's help, Coolidge won the 1924 election.

Even though Bernays saw the power of propaganda during the war and used it to sell products during peacetime, he couldn't have imagined that his writings on public relations would become a tool of the Third Reich.

In the 1920s, Joseph Goebbels became an avid admirer of Bernays and his writings even though Bernays was a Jew. When Goebbels became the minister of propaganda for the Third Reich, he sought to exploit Bernays' ideas to the fullest extent possible. For example, he created a "Fuhrer cult" around Adolph Hitler.

Bernays learned that the Nazis were using his work in 1933, from a foreign correspondent for Hearst newspapers. He later recounted in his 1965 autobiography:

They were using my books as the basis for a destructive campaign against the Jews of Germany. This shocked me, but I knew any human activity could be used for social purposes or misused for antisocial ones.

Goebbels used Bernay's techniques in the mantra that stipulates "The art of propaganda lies in repeating a lie over and over again until it becomes common knowledge."

Propaganda was one of the most important tools the Nazis used to shape the beliefs and attitudes of the German public. Through posters, film, radio, museum exhibits, and other media, they bombarded the German public with messages designed to build support for and gain acceptance of their vision for the future of Germany.

Hitler and Goebbels did not invent propaganda. The word itself was coined by the Catholic Church to describe its efforts to discredit Protestant teachings in the 1600s. Over the years, almost every nation has used propaganda to unite its people in wartime.

Whether or not propaganda was truthful or tasteful was irrelevant to the Nazis. Goebbels wrote in his diary, "No one can say your propaganda is too rough, too mean; these are not criteria by which it may be characterised. It ought not to be decent nor ought it be gentle or soft or humble; it ought to lead to success."

In *Mein Kampf* Hitler wrote: "To achieve its purpose propaganda must keep to a very few points and must harp on theses in slogans until the last member of the public understands what you want him to understand by your slogan. As soon as you sacrifice this slogan and try to be many-sided the effect will piddle away."

Today we might call what Bernays pioneered a form of branding, but at its core, it represents little more than a particularly brazen set of techniques to manipulate people to get them to do your bidding. Its underlying purpose, in large part, is to make money. By convincing people that they want something they do not need, Bernays sought to turn citizens and neighbours into consumers who use their purchasing power to propel themselves down the road to happiness.

Without a moral compass, however, such a transformation promotes a patronising and ultimately cynical view of human nature and human possibilities, one as likely to destroy lives as to build them up.

Donald Trump, king of propaganda was already a master of the art of lies leading up to the 2016 election when he gained the presidency for the first time. Trump, It is the single most vexing question tripping up even the brightest of minds of a generation: how did a billionaire reality television star from New York—one who calls for banning all Muslims and barricading the country behind a big wall to keep "rapists" from Mexico away—managed to elevate himself to the top of the 2016 Republican heap? The rapid ascent of Donald Trump into the hearts and minds of the American people, despite, or perhaps because of, his xenophobia, vulgarity, and misogyny, is enough to question the purity and sanity of those hearts and minds.

Trump's rise can best be explained as a successful marketing campaign. To voters, he has branded himself as an anti-politician politician. He says what some people *want* to say but feel they can't. He wins, all the time, constantly; in fact, he has the most successful propaganda machine since Joseph Goebbels's propaganda methodology of Nazism and faithfulness to its leader Adolf Hitler. Despite multiple high-profile, ugly divorces, Trump has painted himself as the consummate family man.

The electorate slurps this all up. They cannot get enough, in fact, and so Trump conquered the media, too, convincing cable and network news to deliver wall-to-wall in its coverage of the candidate. Trump won't do an in-studio interview, but he *will* call in on a crackly phone line for a few minutes? Blow the whole show up and put it at the top of the prime-time hour. Trump is running late to his 700th press conference, and the shot is just a bunch of people in a room checking their phones? Stay on it. People are beating the snot out of each other at a rally, again? Think of the overnight numbers!

By all accounts, Trump has the nation rapt and the media wrapped around his short fingers. But Trump has been successful and self-serving manipulating the press for decades, long before he entered the political arena. As The Washington Post reported: "…for a decade starting in the 1980s, Trump sometimes assumed a fake name and pretended to be a spokesman representing himself when the media pressed him or he wanted to craft a deliberate message without connecting his name to it."

Reporters at the time quoted a "John Barron" when Trump destroyed a pair of Art Deco friezes that the Metropolitan Museum of Art had wanted to preserve in 1980. (Three days later, he gave *The New York Times* an interview under his name and claimed he had not given an interview sooner because he had been unavailable and out of town.) Barron appeared again in the press when the plans for a Trump Castle in New York came undone, and again that year, when he decided to sell a Madison Avenue property he had planned to develop. It was a trick Trump learned from his father, Fred Trump, who sometimes adopted the moniker "Mr. Green" when dealing with the press, Trump biographer Michael D'Antonio notes, according to the *Post*. It wasn't until Trump went to court in 1990 over his employment of undocumented Polish workers that "Barron" was exposed. "I believe on occasion I used that name," Trump said under oath.

Trump the candidate now has other people to do his messaging— a task that has fallen largely on campaign manager Corey Lewandowski, who has perhaps taken some of the dirty tricks his boss perfected too close to heart. As Politico reported last week, Lewandowski allegedly grabbed a Breitbart reporter, leaving her bruised. He has been accused of manhandling reporters before and making inappropriate comments to female journalists on the campaign trail, cursing at Trump staffers, and threatening Fox News' Megyn Kelly. (A new Buzz feed report adds drunken, late-night calls to female journalists to the unseemly mix.) He has also helped Trump manage to get across a message that resonates, much as "Barron" did for Trump three decades ago. It may not be honest. It may be offensive and aggressive. But to Trump, it's a winning formula, which seems to be all that matters.

Whilst the biggest stumbling block to the globalist policies of the Democratic Party is Trump's campaign to seem at least on the surface be his undying slogan: "Make America Great Again, ' the tradition of individual freedom and the right to own firearms still stands as a pledge on both sides of the political divide. However, national politicians recognise that America is divided down the middle as a republic, for it is now an empire of totalitarian policy be it Democrat or Republican. It is an empire that may be called a new Reich.

We cannot blame Trump for his stance in breathing down the value system of modern America. It has been those fascist globalists. on the right and the left, who behind the scenes have been breaking up the United States into divisions of race, sex, age, generation and culture. This has led to the degrading of education the steady flow of illegal immigrants and fragmentation of the populace on matters such as abortion. Non-heterosexual relationships, and foreign policy. The controls that have been steadily implemented over diminishing the national economy, and corporate downsizing have created undue strain on workers, slowly eroding the nuclear family and moral values. So whether Trump is lying or not is not what at liaise, it is Democracy that no longer is working. Trump like Hitler in his day has picked an ideal time to rise again. His will may not just be a President Trump for a second term of people's rights but a powerful force that will undermine what is left of democracy in America; a dictatorship that will take away the rights of the people and bring about the end of free world democracy in the long term.

CHAPTER 21

EPILOGUE

Father Alois Shicklgurber, in his newfound state of grace, sat by the window of his studio overlooking the Vatican courtyard reading a Bible, with his attention on references in the Book of Revelation, noting the parallels of passages John the Baptist reportedly referred to of end times in his visions of the future. The page references passages seemingly linked to the happenings of today. Fr. Alois cast his eye over Revelation 12:13: and saw The Beast out of the Sea with its ten horns and seven heads that to him resembled those who controlled world power and money flow. He noted that the beast that John the Baptist saw had the head of a leopard that today is symbolic of India, and it had the feet of a bear, that symbolises Russia, and the mouth of a lion that represents the British Empire. The dragon being China gave the beast its powered throne and great authority over mankind.

The priest noted that one of the seven heads of the beast was mortally wounded and then recovered and the whole world was astonished and began to listen to the wounded one, who was in the form of an American President, the seventh head of the beast. He noted from that day forth the world worshipped the dragon, as China had given authority to the beast. It was then the elites lined up all the world's governments under their authority to formalise the final solution of a One World Order. The priest believed there would be but one voice across the airwaves and the television screens of the world that mankind would listen to and obey when the American election is 'Fait accompli' in November and that voice could well be Donald Trump.

[For the beast was given a mouth to utter proud words, to blaspheme and put itself above its master. For in the vision of John the Baptist, he had studied it all before, and he knew the world was heading for Armageddon and it was coming soon.] Book of Revelations.

America is employing form within and In the light of reality, the signs of end times in the Middle East, Russia and Ukraine and the increase of nuclear arms around the borders of North Korea, with Russian troops on one border, and China's weaponry on another make for a tender box ready to explode worldwide. South Korea is facing off on the southern border against the biggest army of foot soldiers in the world right now in North Korea. It seems that the Korean Peninsula may be the final straw in the race against time to starve off a nuclear World War. and a final Armageddon. And if Trump wins then who knows how he will view these matters that could be of critical consequence. for America and mankind.

I intended to delay the completion of this chapter until after the election but I see no reason to delay in releasing it now. It may well influence you the reader of the USA to cast your vote looking at your leaders in a different light based on the content of this book.

Last week Robert F Kennedy Jr's decision to endorse Donald Trump will hearten Republicans, despite Kamala Harris and Tim Walz enjoying a triumphant Democratic National Convention (DNC). The decision of the former Democratic president's nephew will be welcomed by Trump, who had been slipping behind Ms Harris in the polls since she replaced Joe Biden at the top of the ticket. With Mr Kennedy polling at around 5 per cent, his endorsement will leave the two candidates running neck and neck.

The Democrats have just pulled off an impressive feat: a flawless, star-studded convention that brought critical viewership just a month after changing their presidential candidate. Ms Harris made the most of her opportunity to re-introduce herself to the American public. It was not an inspiring speech, but one shrewdly calculated to neutralise her weaknesses. Time will tell how effective it was, but for now, Ms Harris is leading in the polls and the fundraising stakes. Trump's torrent of tweets during her address suggests he has been rattled. Ms Harris continues to outperform Trump in both poll numbers and political donations, and the

DNC had an energy that was lacking from the Republican convention last month.

At the moment, she has momentum in this race, and while she did not seize the opportunity to set out a grand vision for America in her convention speech, she did enough to keep her party happy. That said, the end of RFK Jr's campaign is likely to be a boost for Trump and there is still plenty of time for this election to be upended once again. Since Mr Biden bowed out, the presidential election has been the Democrats' to lose. All Ms Harris needed to do was announce a sensible set of policies to reassure Americans that she has abandoned her formerly quite extreme Leftist positions: defunding the police, the Green New Deal, sanctuary cities – you name a barmy idea, she's backed it in the past.

But Ms Harris hasn't said anything, and people are starting to notice. If she does not do something about this, she will take a hit. The other thing Ms Harris needed to do was choose a vice-presidential candidate who would counterbalance her image as an elite liberal lawyer from San Francisco. On the face of it, Mr Walz is a good fit: teacher, coach, and National Guard service as a top sergeant, not an officer. But there is also the matter of almost two decades in office as Minnesota governor and US congressman: Mr Walz is a big-city political operator, not a small-town man at all and his voting record smells of California, not the Nebraska prairie

If Ms Harris and Mr Walz cannot make themselves more appealing to centrist swing voters, and Trump can avoid committing any more of his trademark egregious blunders, he might just win this thing.

Indeed, the Democrats have made a convincing play for the title of the patriotic party, with Mr Walz's folksy references to family, faith and flag pairing nicely with a generally moderate platform of speakers - Bernie Sanders, once a populist darling, spoke to a crowd that could hardly hide their yawns. But the Democrats are not out of the woods yet. Ms Harris's new candidate boost shouldn't take away from the fact this is still an incredibly tight race. Bill Clinton's quiet warning against overconfidence may prove prophetic for this new, still-untested nominee.

Trump is, was and always will be a salesman first. He only dealt with politics as a way to make money for his business. He floated the idea of running for Mayor and Governor of New York at different times before he talked about running for President. He was talking about this for many years and would always pull out before he had to commit. The circumstances in 2016 were such that he felt he could get the maximum publicity for his business so he filed to run, never expecting that he would win. The longer he lasted in the election, the more publicity. That was the goal. No one in the Republican primaries knew what to do with him. He didn't behave in a rational, political way. One by one they all gave up. He was the last man standing. His stunt was working better than he expected. Then the night of the election, lightning struck. His sales pitch was so effective he sold everyone beyond his dreams. Then the nightmare began. And here he is back with the same rhetoric as his first term.

Trump said he'd want to be a dictator on his first day in office. His supporters cheered the idea, but that wouldn't come to fruition. What might come instead is an authoritarian presidency punishing opponents and rewarding allies, overhauling government to serve his whims, not the country's. And all of it obscured by a web of dishonesty. It's what he's said he'll do and it's what his allies are working to ensure he can do.

About the Author.

Doug McPhillips, poet, singer, songwriter, and author, commenced his journey of discovery over a decade ago after life-changing experiences.
The many tracks he has traversed throughout the Northern Hemisphere and down under in New Zealand and Australia have resulted in the facts and fiction of this novel.

Doug has recorded and sung songs interrelated to this work majestic melodies in an authentic Australian style.

Doug has written twenty-one novels, including two books of poems, a travel guide, and three albums of his songs, all inspired by his adventurers.

www.caminoway.com.au
__" A journey of the Spirit."

Doug is an adventurer who divides his time between creative pursuits, family and friends, and those who may benefit most from his efforts and experience.

www.ingramcontent.com/pod-product-compliance
Lightning Source LLC
Chambersburg PA
CBHW061805290426
44109CB00031B/2943